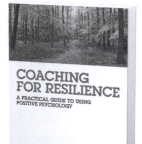

Coaching for Resilience

A practical guide to using positive psychology

Adrienne Green and
John Humphrey

Publisher's note

Every possible effort has been made to ensure that the information contained in this book is accurate at the time of going to press, and the publishers and authors cannot accept responsibility for any errors or omissions, however caused. No responsibility for loss or damage occasioned to any person acting, or refraining from action, as a result of the material in this publication can be accepted by the editor, the publisher or either of the authors.

First published in Great Britain and the United States in 2012 by Kogan Page Limited

120 Pentonville Road	1518 Walnut Street, Suite 1100	4737/23 Ansari Road
London N1 9JN	Philadelphia PA 19102	Daryaganj
United Kingdom	USA	New Delhi 110002
www.koganpage.com		India

© Adrienne Green and John Humphrey

ISBN   978 0 7494 6645 9
E-ISBN 978 0 7494 6646 6

British Library Cataloguing-in-Publication Data

A CIP record for this book is available from the British Library.

Library of Congress Cataloging-in-Publication Data

Green, Adrienne.
    Coaching for resilience : a practical guide to using positive psychology / Adrienne Green, John Humphrey. – 1st ed.
        p. cm.
    Includes bibliographical references.
    ISBN 978-0-7494-6645-9 – ISBN 978-0-7494-6646-6   1. Resilience (Personality trait)
2. Positive psychology.   I. Green, Adrienne.   II. Title.
    BF698.35.R47H86 2012
    155.2'4–dc23

                                                            2012012305

Typeset by Graphicraft Limited, Hong Kong
Printed and bound in India by Replika Press Pvt Ltd

CONTENTS

ABOUT THE AUTHORS

Adrienne Green

Adrienne practised for many years as a psychotherapist and psychotherapy supervisor within both private and National Health mental health care services. In particular she worked with people suffering with severe stress, anxiety and depression. Since then she has worked as a consultant, trainer and coach within both private and public sector organizations specializing in stress management, resilience building, management of change and conflict resolution. Adrienne is the author of *Out of the blue: A practical guide to overcoming and preventing depression*.

John Humphrey

John was formerly head of the Employment Risk Consulting practice of Marsh UK, and advises many leading employers on health and employment issues. He has run the health care functions of Procter and Gamble and the Beecham Group. Together with Lord Robens he founded BMI Occupational Health. John was the founding Managing Director of Minerva Health Management and the Chairman of Marsh Health. His books include *Looking After Corporate Health: A guide to protecting the health and productivity of people in the business environment*, and *Fast Track to the Top: 10 skills for career success*.

Adrienne and John are the founding directors of Nice Work Consulting Ltd. Nice Work is a company that specializes in workplace psychology and employee well-being and provides consultancy, training and coaching services to many private sector companies, as well as public sector organizations including local authorities and NHS Trusts. Further information about Nice Work is available on the website **www.niceworkconsulting.co.uk**. You are also very welcome to contact the authors by e-mail at **info@niceworkconsulting.co.uk**.

ACKNOWLEDGEMENTS

We'd like to thank the hundreds of people we have worked with over the years for all they have taught us along the way. Thanks also to the philosophers, psychologists and other authors, both ancient and modern, whom we have mentioned in this book for their wisdom and inspiration. A special thank you to Una McGrath for her encouragement, very welcome tea breaks and painstaking corrections, and to Martina O'Sullivan for her expert guidance. Finally, Adrienne would like to give her most heartfelt thanks to her husband, writer George Green, for his endless love, patience and support, and his invaluable suggestions and advice in the writing of this book.

Introduction

Welcome to our guide to Coaching for Resilience. Whether you are seeking to build your own personal resilience, or to help others to achieve theirs, we hope you will find this as powerful and enjoyable a learning experience as the hundreds of people we ourselves have trained and coached over our many years of experience in this field.

Why you need to read this book

Health

In an increasingly complex and demanding world, lack of resilience leads people to become much more vulnerable to stress. In turn, stress can lead people to suffer from psychological conditions such as anxiety, panic attacks and depression, as well as physical effects ranging from frequent colds and coughs to high blood pressure and heart disease.

Work

There are many studies that show stress to be the number one cause of sickness absence in the workplace. Whether you work in HR (Human Resources), or as a team leader or manager, a sound grasp of the ways that you can help yourself and your colleagues to maintain and even build their resilience will reduce the likelihood that you yourself will suffer, or that you will lose valuable members of your team, as a result of stress-related illness.

Everyday life

But, of course, stress isn't confined to the workplace. People also have to deal with relationship, family, home, finance and health issues on a daily basis. As an individual you need to have a high level of resilience to manage the many and sometimes competing demands you have to juggle each day.

As a coach, trainer or consultant, you also need to have the knowledge and ability to educate and motivate others to build the resilience they need to survive and thrive in a challenging world.

What this book contains

Most people would agree that resilience is a beneficial quality to have. But, what exactly is it? Where does it come from? How can you build and maintain resilience in the face of the pressures and demands that confront you each day? This book will give you the in-depth answers to all these questions and more.

Our approach has been to combine our own ideas and strategies with those presented by popular and well-respected writers such as Steven Covey, Daryl Conner and Eckhart Tolle. We wanted to provide what you might call a 'one-stop-shop' handbook that would give you a deep understanding of resilience and the tools you need to build that crucial yet often elusive quality. Out of the wide range of theories and techniques we have explored and used over the years, we have distilled the seven that have had the most immediate impact and lasting effect for ourselves and the people we have worked with. These are the 7 KEYS that form the core of this book.

Within you will find clear, detailed and structured explanations of the principles of positive psychology, along with practical exercises to work through and reflect upon as we:

- define resilience, and explore its origins and qualities;
- define stress, and show how it undermines resilience;
- explore why it is so important to build resilience;
- explore the two underlying psychological dynamics that cause stress;
- reveal the 7 KEYS to Building Resilience for Life.

Throughout the book there are anecdotes and examples that show how these apply at work and in everyday home life.

We hope you will enjoy the following discussions and exercises, and of course our 7 KEYS. We hope that you will find them informative, thought-provoking and inspiring. Most of all we hope you will use and practise what you discover here to enhance your resilience and make a real difference in your life.

How to use this book – advice for all readers

Take your time

We often present the content of this book to groups of people at a live workshop or training course. During these sessions the ideas we explore arise one after another as people discuss topics and work through the exercises together. We've found that this gradual step-by-step process has the greatest impact. We would like you to have the same powerful learning experience as those who attend our courses in person. So we would encourage you to resist the temptation to flick through or turn the pages to find the answers or see what is coming next. You have the luxury of being able to work through the presentations and exercises at your own pace. Take it slowly and let the ideas unfold and build on each other one at a time.

Keep an open mind

Approach this book with an open mind. You don't have to agree with everything we say. We only ask that you give our suggestions some careful thought. Reflect on how the different ideas relate (or don't relate) to you and your own life, and be honest in your responses. Also, you don't have to find everything we offer here helpful in order to benefit from the book. You might discover just one thing from the whole book, perhaps one thought or one KEY, that will change your life, and that will be enough. Adopt and practise what you find most relevant and useful.

Explore and experiment

You might be tempted just to glance over the exercises and not actually do them. But learning is deepest and most effective when people explore a subject actively and attentively. So we would strongly encourage you to engage with the exercises as fully as you can. This is a great opportunity for you to get to know and understand yourself, and to develop your personal skills and qualities. So do put plenty of thought and effort into this programme. Then you will get the most out of it.

Advice for coaches, trainers, consultants, managers, etc

This section comes after our advice for all readers because we feel, and are sure you would agree, that the first step for anyone who aims to facilitate the personal development of others is to absorb ideas and apply techniques and strategies to themselves. As a guide or mentor for others, you know that you require a high degree of self-awareness and self-development to have the confidence and conviction you need to gain the trust of the people you work with. If you yourself are enthusiastic as a result of the successful application of ideas and strategies, you will inspire enthusiasm in others. They will be more likely to collaborate constructively with you, and to put in the effort they need to succeed if they feel assured of your belief in the approaches you suggest to them.

So, to begin with, we would recommend that you follow the suggestions above that we would make to any individual who is reading this book for their own understanding and development. When you are familiar with the ideas and exercises contained here, you will be able to put forward relevant questions or ideas to clients, staff, etc, and use the appropriate exercises. In our own practice we have either worked through sections of the book or appropriate KEYS with people, or set these as 'homework' for reflection and discussion at a later date.

Really, there are as many ways to use this book as there are facilitators who engage with it. Each individual practitioner or manager will have their own particular approach and each client or group will bring their unique interests and needs. As you would with any approach, the crucial thing is, as always, to listen. The person you are working with will tell you what they need, and when.

Our approach to building resilience

Our approach is to develop an understanding of the psychology of resilience. In particular we will explore the deep psychological processes that undermine resilience and make it difficult for people to enhance their resilience, or sometimes even to maintain it. Once you understand why you sometimes lack resilience then you can work out how to interrupt and prevent those undermining psychological processes and allow your resilience to grow.

It may seem rather negative to approach this topic from a perspective that looks at what undermines resilience! Why do we take this kind of psychological approach? How will it benefit you to understand the topic from this point of view?

To answer these questions we need to re-introduce a concept that we touched on right at the start of our Introduction; that is the concept of stress. We have realized that there is a very close relationship between resilience and stress, which we can best describe as a 'vicious circle'.

A vicious circle

Earlier we said that we want to help people build resilience so they can manage difficult times in life without becoming overwhelmed and possibly mentally and physically unwell. Why would a lack of resilience cause people to become mentally and physically unwell?

The reason is that, without resilience, people respond to difficult situations in life by becoming stressed; and we know that stress can lead to many psychological, emotional and physical symptoms that can be very unpleasant and even dangerous to health. We will look at this in much greater detail later. For now we'll just make the general point that it takes energy and well-being to maintain resilience. When people are stressed they become exhausted and ill. So, the effects of stress undermine people's resilience.

When people's resilience is lowered by the effects of stress, they are likely to respond to further challenges by becoming even more stressed. That lowers resilience more, which leads to more stress, which leads to even lower resilience, which leads to more stress... and so on... in a vicious circle, something like this:

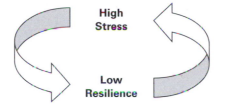

**High
Stress**

**Low
Resilience**

Whether this circle starts with low resilience or with high stress depends on the individual person. You might be a person who is generally quite resilient, but a period of severe difficulty could cause even you to become stressed. The effects of this stress will undermine your natural resilience. Then you'll have less resilience to respond to future events, which will lead to even higher levels of stress... which will lower your resilience even further... etc. In this case your 'vicious circle' starts with stress.

Or, you might be a person whose resilience is low to begin with. This means that you become stressed quite easily. Every time you become stressed, the effects of this will lower your resilience levels even further and this will make you more and more vulnerable to stress. In this case your 'vicious circle' starts with low resilience.

For the purposes of this book, it doesn't really matter where your circle starts. What matters is how you avoid getting into it, or once you are in it, how to get out of it.

How to avoid or get out of the vicious circle

There are two possible ways we could approach this.

1. Increase your resilience

One approach is for us to try to give you more resilience. If we could do that you would be able to keep out of the circle simply by having extremely high levels of resilience and not getting stressed. The difficulty with this approach is that, if you think about it, it is actually impossible to impart resilience in a book. Yes, we know, that's not a very encouraging start to a book that is supposed to show you how to build resilience! But bear with us for a moment.

It is not possible to impart resilience in a book because resilience is a 'quality'. It is part of a person's personality. Resilience isn't something that people 'do'; it is something that they 'are'. Where do people who are resilient get that quality from? Are they born with it? Do they develop it through experience? Does it grow through their relationships with others over time? Could it be that it comes from a combination of all of these? Whatever the answer, it is not possible for us to give you these things in a book. We can't 'make' you born with it, and we can't give you the experiences or the relationships that you need to learn it over time.

So what can we do to help you build and maintain your resilience?

2. Lower your stress

The other approach is to show you how to prevent your resilience from being undermined by stress; that is, to show you how to keep your stress levels as low as possible. If we could do that you would be able to keep out of the circle by making sure that you suffer as little as possible from stress and its damaging effects. The good news is that we can do this. That's because to be able to manage stress isn't a 'quality' like resilience. Rather, it is an 'ability'. Unlike resilience, managing stress is not something that people 'are'; it is something that they 'do'. Even if someone is so good at managing stress that it appears to be a natural gift, the truth is that they are doing something that enables them to avoid stress when they are confronted with difficulties. We believe we know what they are doing. We believe we can show you how to do it, and that you can get good at it too, by practising the techniques and strategies we'll describe to you.

So this is the approach we will take. We'll give you the tools you need to keep your stress levels low, no matter what challenges or difficulties you might have to face. That way, if you are a naturally resilient person you'll be able to maintain the resilience you already have. You might even be able to build it up even more. If you lack resilience at the moment, you'll be able to build that up over time as it won't be constantly undermined by stress that you currently find difficult to manage.

It's a stress course!

Now you might be thinking, 'Ah right, it's really a stress management course – lots of breathing exercises, dolphin music and advice to eat lettuce. I know all that stuff!'

Well, yes and no. Yes, we are going to work on the topic from the angle of managing stress. No, there won't be any breathing exercises, dolphin music or lettuce.

Traditional methods such as breathing techniques, massage, going for long walks, listening to soothing music, eating healthily, etc can be very valuable in maintaining physical well-being and reducing feelings of anxiety or even panic. We wouldn't want to discourage anyone from using these. However, we will not be taking time to look at them in any great depth in this book. This is for two reasons.

The first is that you're right; you do know all that stuff. Also, there are already plenty of books, DVDs and websites that contain that kind of inform-ation and we're sure you don't need us to add to those here.

The second is this. We believe that, most often, these methods merely keep stress at bay and reduce symptoms in the short term. If you are using massage, breathing exercises and soothing music to 'calm down' when you are feeling stressed out then we would say this is not stress management, it is 'damage limitation'.

As we've said, that can be very valuable sometimes. However, you need to manage stress in ways that will have a more profound and enduring effect if you want to build high levels of long-lasting resilience. You need to manage it in ways that remove the need to 'calm down' or 'limit the damage' because you won't become stressed in the first place. Our 7 KEYS will help you achieve this because they tackle stress where it begins. They tackle stress at a deep psychological level.

Easier said than done, but worth it

We should be honest now and warn you that you might find these KEYS quite difficult to do. We know this because sometimes it is still hard even for us to put them into practice when we are under a lot of pressure, or when life events are difficult or painful. We also know it from the feedback we get from people who attend our sessions. The comment we most often hear from our delegates is 'Yes, but that's easier said than done!'

It's true. The KEYS are easy to say, and difficult to do. The reason for this will become clear as we reveal them to you. You'll find they often challenge your instinctive behaviour patterns and your habitual ways of responding to other people or situations. In other words, the KEYS get you out of your 'comfort zone'.

To succeed in your goal of building resilience you will need to be willing and courageous enough to give the KEYS a go even if it means you have to step out of your 'comfort zone'. We know these KEYS are challenging, but we can promise you three things:

1 they become easier with practice;

2 they work; and

3 it will be worth it!

PART ONE
Essential foundations for lasting resilience

Defining 'resilience' and 'stress'

So far we've been talking about 'resilience' and 'stress' as if we could take it for granted that we all mean the same things by those words. That isn't necessarily the case. When we ask people in our groups to define resilience and stress, they often come up with meanings that are close to or the same as our own; but sometimes they are quite different, especially with the word 'resilience'.

Obviously we will be making lots of suggestions about 'managing stress' and 'building resilience' throughout this book. If you have a different view from us about what we are trying to help you manage and build then you might find our approach a bit confusing. So before we go any further we should define exactly what *we* mean by these terms so that our goals and approach will make sense to you.

Resilience

1. What is resilience?

We'd like to give you a chance to think about your own definition of 'resilience' before we reveal the one that we are using for this book. You'll find that ours is taken from a dictionary. But, rather than go to a dictionary right away yourself, it would be interesting to explore your own personal sense of what 'resilience' means.

To find your own definition it might help to think about people whom you would say are resilient. Could you name a famous person you regard as resilient?

Write their name here ....

Could you name someone you know personally whom you think is resilient?

Write their name here ....

Now write down a few words or short phrases that describe these people and why you think they are resilient.

....

....

....

....

We have found that the famous people most often named in this exercise are Margaret Thatcher and Nelson Mandela. The reason people give for pointing to Margaret Thatcher is that she was mentally and emotionally 'strong'. She took tough decisions, stuck to her own views and was unmoved by criticism. The reason they give for identifying Nelson Mandela is that, despite many years of imprisonment and isolation, he came back with re-newed energy and an inspirational vision for the future of his country.

You may not have named Mrs Thatcher or Mr Mandela specifically as your famous person, but did you write down any of the qualities above to describe them? People in our groups most commonly note either 'strength' or 'the ability to bounce back' as the key features of resilience. We would agree with one of these.

Our definition of resilience

In the strict dictionary definition of resilience, 'strength' is not the crucial aspect of resilience. Much more important is the 'ability to bounce back'. In fact the definition from the *Shorter Oxford English Dictionary* is:

1 The act of rebounding or springing back; rebound, recoil.
2 Elasticity; the power of resuming the original shape or position after compression, bending etc.

This is what we mean when we talk about 'resilience' in this book. It is not the same as strength, which enables you to remain calm, unaffected, or 'stony' in the face of life's difficulties and challenges. Rather it is that you are moved emotionally by those difficulties – you feel pain, anxiety, fear, sadness, even despair – and then *can recover to your original state*.

At its best resilience enables a person to recover to an even more re-sourceful state. This happens when the person can use a difficult experience to become more aware of their personal qualities, skills and abilities, and is able to use those more readily and fully when they are challenged again in the future.

So it is possible for a person to be strong and yet not very resilient. A strong person is like a rock; hard, tough and unbending. That rock won't be pushed or pulled out of shape by pressure, but hard knocks can chip away at it and once it is chipped it stays chipped. It might take a very powerful hit to break it completely but when it is broken it cannot put itself back together again. This is not our goal for you.

A person who is resilient may not appear to be very strong. That's because they bend and give way. They react to what happens to them emotionally and physically. They are like an elastic band that can be pulled, stretched, twisted and scrunched – but then will go back to its original shape when it is let go.

Of course it is possible to break an elastic band. You could stretch it beyond its flexibility until it snaps, or pull at it repeatedly until it loses its elasticity and can be broken easily. In the same way, even very resilient people have their limits. The truth is that everyone can be broken by events that are beyond endurance for them.

Our goal is to work with you to build the power and toughness of your resilience. We want you to be like an elastic band that is extremely thick and strong so it will be very difficult for life to stretch you beyond your breaking point.

You might be pulled out of shape by life events. By this we mean you may become very emotional at times. You might need to seek help. Or you might need to withdraw and take some time out for a while. But then you will come back with new vitality and resolve, just like Nelson Mandela.

2.   Where does resilience come from?

We touched on this question earlier when we explained our approach to building resilience. There we offered these possible answers:

- that people are born with it;
- that they develop it through experience or relationships over time;
- that it might be a combination of these two.

This is a question that psychologists are still exploring and, to be perfectly honest, we don't know the answer. It might be in the genes and you have a set level of resilience at birth. But we know that, with time and experience, people change and they develop greater ability to recover from setbacks. We also know that people who are very resilient can be pulled and pushed by events to such an extent that they seem to give up and become unable to recover from difficult times – their elastic gets overstretched. So a person's degree of resilience does seem to have more of a link with life experience. Perhaps it is a combination of genes and experience.

One possibility we haven't considered yet is that resilience is learnt. We might be able to discover something about this by looking at another psychological concept; depression. Depression seems to run in families so researchers used to believe that it was probably mostly genetic. But then some psychologists started to ask whether the reason it runs in families is not so much because of genes but more because it is being taught and learnt within those families. The idea is that children learn to react to life in a depressed way by watching and copying their depressed parents, siblings, uncles and aunts, etc.

So could it be that people who lack resilience learnt to be that way as children by copying inflexible, brittle attitudes and behaviour? Could it be that people who are very resilient learnt that by copying flexible, bounce-back types of attitudes and behaviour? Also, children respond very strongly to being rewarded and punished; praised or scolded. Perhaps resilient and non-resilient behaviour is learnt through this process too.

Where do you think you got your resilience (or lack of resilience) from?

Do you think that you were just born that way? Are you and other members of your family similar in ability to recover from misfortunes? Would you relate your levels of resilience to childhood learning or more to life experiences over time? Do you feel that your life experiences have led you to become more or less resilient over the course of your life? Has your 'elastic' been stretched so often that it has lost its springiness and ability to bounce back? Or has it become thicker and tougher?

Whatever your answers are to these questions, as we said in our introductory section, it isn't possible for us to give you the quality of resilience by what we write in this book. We can't give you the genes and we can't give you the childhood relationships or life experiences that you would have needed to develop it over time.

However, we did suggest that there is another angle we can use to build resilience. We can help you to stop your resilience being undermined constantly until it is like that overstretched elastic band. Our theory is that the major factor that undermines resilience is stress. We can teach you how to manage stress in a powerful and long-lasting way so your resilience will be allowed to grow and strengthen.

Stress

What is stress?

Q. It is often said that a little bit of stress is a good thing. Do you think
    that is:

TRUE?   or   FALSE?

How you responded to that question is likely to depend on your view of
what stress does to a person.

If you said TRUE, that's probably because you believe stress gives people
an adrenalin rush that helps them to be focused, motivated and up for
a challenge. You might think people need that bit of stress to feel excited,
to bring out their best performance, or maybe even just to get up in the
morning. People who believe that a little bit of stress is a good thing are
afraid that being 'calm' all the time would lead to apathy. They believe they
might not be bothered to do anything because they just wouldn't care.

If you said FALSE it's likely to be because you feel that it is important to
be motivated, energized and focused in your life, but that that's different
from being stressed. You believe that once a person becomes stressed then
things have begun to become too much to deal with and the experience has
started to become unpleasant and unhealthy.

At the risk of alienating a lot of readers at this very early stage of our
book, we have to say we would agree with those who responded FALSE to
our question.

We are completely in favour of people being full of energy, passionate and
focused. We would agree that the buzz of an adrenalin rush helps people to
rise to a challenge. We, too, don't want people to be calm all the time. We want
people to be able to get angry sometimes. There are lots of things to get
angry about in life; injustice, poverty, war, discrimination, abuse, dishonesty,
etc. If no one got angry about those things then nothing would change. We
want people to be able to be sad. It would be unnatural and unhealthy not
to grieve when you lose something that is precious to you. We also want
people to be thrilled, excited and joyously happy when great things happen.

It is important to understand that stress isn't the only experience that brings
about the release of adrenalin. All of the emotions mentioned above happen
with adrenalin, even the positive ones, and you don't need to be stressed to feel
them. In fact, all stress does is undermine positive emotions such as happiness and excitement and increase the pain of the more difficult emotions
such as anger, sadness and grief. That's because, wherever there is stress,
there is an added ingredient. Our definition will reveal that ingredient.

Our definition of stress

As you can imagine, the definition provided by the *Shorter Oxford English Dictionary* goes on for quite a few paragraphs to take into account all of the various contexts in which people use the word 'stress'. The bit that is relevant to us is where it defines stress as:

> The overpowering pressure of some adverse force or influence.

For us, the important word in this definition is the word 'overpowering'. Pressure is fine. In fact, when people say they think a little bit of stress is a good thing, it often turns out they mean a bit of pressure is a good thing. They mean it is pressure that gives them the buzz of challenge and excitement they need to be at their most effective. And we would absolutely agree with that.

However, in our definition, pressure becomes stress when that pressure has become overpowering. In other words, the pressure has become more than they can cope with. When that happens, the effects of the pressure on the person have become more negative than positive.

So, the definition we use when we present our courses is this:

> Stress is the condition experienced when someone perceives that they are *unable to meet the demands placed* upon them.

In other words:

> People get stressed when they have a sense that they are *unable to cope*.

These are different words from the dictionary definition, but the meaning is the same. Stress is not about being challenged or under pressure. It is about being unable to meet demands and unable to cope with that pressure.

So far so good? But there's more.

There are other words in our definitions that we believe are even more important than the ones we've italicised. These other words are at the heart of the definition of stress that we use as the basis for our approach to managing stress.

Look at the definitions again and see if you can identify what those words are.

Underline or highlight them here before you read on.

> Stress is the condition experienced when someone perceives that they are *unable to meet the demands* placed upon them.

And in this one?

> People get stressed when they have a sense that they are *unable to cope*.

(The answers are on the next page so you wouldn't see them before you selected the words yourself...)

Did you identify these words?

Stress is the condition experienced when someone perceives that they are *unable to meet the demands* placed upon them.

In other words;

People get stressed when they have a sense that they are *unable to cope*.

The words 'perceives' and 'sense' are crucial here. A 'perception' or a 'sense' of something is not reality; or at least not necessarily reality. It is a personal, subjective experience of reality. It's the way that someone sees something or thinks about something from their own point of view.

Stress and perception

There are three things you need to understand about perceptions and how they relate to stress:

1 Perceptions might be true reflections of how your world really is, and equally they might not be.
A person could become stressed because they sense that they are unable to cope and they are right; they truly are unable to cope. But equally they could become stressed if they sense that they can't cope and they are wrong; they really can cope.

2 Perceptions can be conscious or unconscious.
You can be consciously aware of your sense of being overwhelmed, and you might even think or say out loud to yourself 'I just can't cope with this anymore'. On the other hand, the perception of being unable to cope might happen at an unconscious level. Your brain might register your sense of being unable to cope before you can be consciously aware of that yourself. It may be that the first indication you have that you are stressed is one or more of the physical, emotional, behavioural or psychological symptoms of stress that we will discuss a bit later.

3 The perception of being unable to cope triggers FEAR.
Fear is the 'added ingredient' we mentioned earlier. Wherever there is stress there is fear, whether you are consciously aware of it or not.

What is that fear about? What are you afraid of when you have a sense that you are unable to cope? Is it that you will fall apart? That your world will crumble? That you will lose everything? Yes, it's possible those are the kinds of thing you fear on a conscious level. But our understanding of stress is that it always starts at an unconscious level. Stress begins at the level of instinct, and that instinct is the instinct for survival. At that level the unconscious fear is that you won't survive.

Fight-or-flight

When the brain perceives that you are unable to cope with a situation, it reacts instinctively (that means without your conscious awareness or choice) as though your life was being threatened. As far as your instinct for survival is concerned, being unable to cope is as much a threat to your life as a physical attack would be, and that instinct for survival reacts in the same way to both – with the fight-or-flight response.

To explain how and why this happens we need to show you how the fight-or-flight response comes about. The next chapter will take you on a brief tour of the inside of the brain. We know you might be tempted to skip this bit if scientific explanations look a bit daunting to you. Please do stay with it though, because what we explain next is crucial background to the 7 KEYS. It really is quite simple, and we're sure you'll be able to identify with the descriptions and examples.

The science bit

How the brain works

If you cut open the human brain you will find that it looks just like this...

Pre-frontal cortex

Hippocampus

Thalamus

Amygdala

Ok, perhaps it doesn't look exactly like this with the major areas helpfully labelled. Obviously this is just a model of the brain, and what follows is a very simplistic outline of an extremely complex process. This is what happens in the brain from the moment a person experiences something in their world to their reaction to what is going on. We'll describe the process in a general way and then link the process to stress.

First there's the sensory thalamus that detects everything you experience through your senses – sight, hearing, touch, taste and smell. It only receives sensations though; it doesn't make any sense of them. So, for example, it registers light and shade but can't recognize those impressions as, say, 'table' or 'flower'. It can register loudness and pitch of a sound but can't tell you that it's, for example, 'music' or 'aeroplane'.

So that we can make sense of the world, the sensory thalamus has to pass the information it receives to the pre-frontal cortex (at the front of the head). The pre-frontal cortex is the part of the brain that can 'think'. It can identify what things are from the jumble of signals it receives from the sensory thalamus.

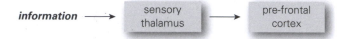

The pre-frontal cortex doesn't do all of this recognition work on its own. Very often it has to get help from another area of the brain, the hippocampus. The hippocampus is the brain's long-term memory store. Once it has begun to piece together signals from the sensory thalamus, the pre-frontal cortex checks with the hippocampus to see if there is anything in its store of memories from past experiences that can help to work out what the signals from the sensory thalamus mean.

All of this activity in the brain has only one purpose: that is, to tell a person how to react to what is happening in their world. People's reactions depend very much on how they feel about things.

So the pre-frontal cortex sends all the information it has gathered to the amygdala. The amygdala is the emotional hub of the brain. When the amygdala is stimulated it starts off a whole set of chemical and hormonal reactions in the brain and body that lead people to feel an emotion. The emotion they feel will determine what they do.

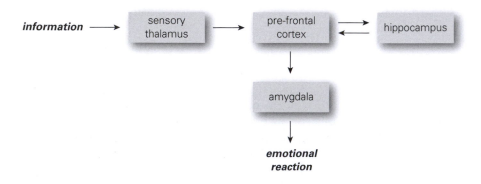

For example, if the brain registers heat or cold, people feel uncomfortable so they'll take action to cool down or warm up. If the brain registers the presence of a friend, people feel relaxed and happy. This leads them to take action to prolong the contact and stay close. If the brain registers a loss, people feel sad. This sadness leads them to a range of possible actions. They might cry, or withdraw or perhaps seek help.

In particular the amygdala has a direct connection with the bit of the brain that sets off the fear reaction, ie the 'fight-or-flight' response. If the brain registers that an enemy is near then people feel threatened and afraid. This leads them to take action to get away from or fight that enemy.

The diagram below shows the whole process from start to finish.

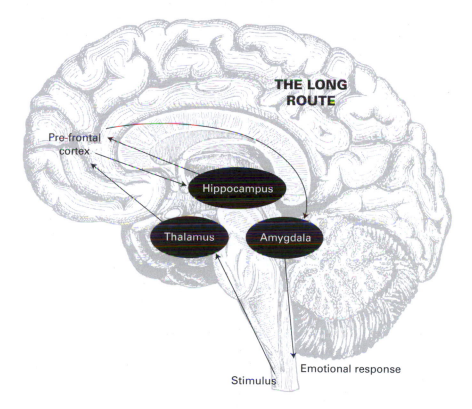

We call this a 'long route' because the signals have to cover a long distance to reach all of these different areas of the brain. Including thinking and decision-making time, the whole journey could take a second or even two.

How the brain works in the real world

That's the scientific theory. Now, how does this work in the real world?

Human beings in modern Western societies such as ours live in a world that is very complicated. They have to deal with advanced technology, frequently changing and competitive working environments, complex financial concerns, family and relationship issues, etc. But the human brain as we've shown it above developed about two hundred thousand years ago – way before any of these aspects of life came into being. It developed to make sense of and react to very different challenges from those faced by people nowadays.

What were the challenges that people faced all those thousands of years ago?

You're probably thinking about things like attacks by animal predators or enemy tribes, and the near constant struggle to find sufficient food and protection from the elements. You'd be right of course. Two hundred thousand years ago the major function of the brain was to help human beings to stay alive. So let's examine how the brain played its part in the most important aspect of human life: survival.

The long route

Imagine that you're out hunting for food in the wilderness of two hundred thousand years ago. Suddenly you hear a rustling sound in front of you and a tiger leaps out from its hiding place in the long grass. You can see it, hear it and smell it. You can feel the warmth of its breath. All of these sensations flood into the sensory thalamus, which sends the signals to the pre-frontal cortex. The pre-frontal cortex begins to work out what is happening. It might check with the hippocampus to see if there are any stored memories of large, striped, fast-moving, snarling things with long, pointed teeth. The pre-frontal cortex can then confirm that this is a man-eating sabre-toothed tiger and that you saw one of them attack and eat another person just last week. It takes account of everything else in your conscious awareness at the time and makes a decision about how to react. Finally it sends messages to the amygdala telling it that you are in extreme danger, that you'd better get very scared and either gear up for a fight or get away fast!

The trouble is, as we've said, all this can take one to two seconds. This is quite long enough for the animal to have pounced and begun to eat you for its lunch.

We're sure you'll agree this is not a very effective way for the brain to ensure a person's survival. Human beings would simply not have lasted two hundred thousand years if that was the way the brain actually worked in response to life-threatening situations. But humans have lasted, and not only for two hundred thousand years. In fact, the history of humankind goes back over four million years. So how did humans manage to survive this long?

They survived because, as the brain developed, it didn't use the long route when a person was under threat. Instead it used a route that takes only one-tenth of a second and it's this:

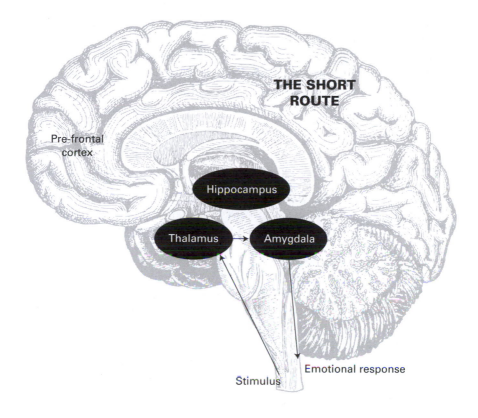

THE SHORT
ROUTE

Pre-frontal
cortex

Hippocampus

Thalamus → Amygdala

Emotional response

Stimulus

The short route

Even though the brain was developing a very sophisticated pre-frontal cortex over the hundreds of thousands of years of human evolution, it continued to use a very primitive process whenever it registered a signal from the outside world that gave it the slightest warning of a threat. This is called the 'short route'. The short route cut out the areas of the brain that think, analyse and reason; areas such as the pre-frontal cortex and the hippocampus. In this route, the amygdala picked up signals flowing through the sensory thalamus before they reached any of these higher functioning parts of the brain.

Whenever the amygdala detected any signals, or patterns of signals, from the sensory thalamus that were the same or similar to those of past danger, it set off the fight-or-flight response without waiting for instructions from the pre-frontal cortex. The human body was ready to act in a fraction of a second and therefore was much more likely to be able to protect itself.

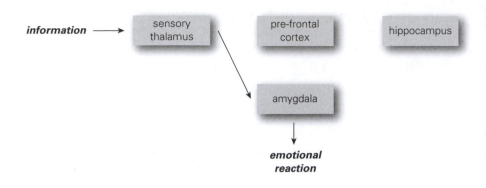

Two important things to note about the short route:

1 In the short route the amygdala reacted only to the sensations it picked up from the sensory thalamus. So, it didn't know what was causing those sensations. It triggered the fight-or-flight response at the merest hint of the sound of a rustle. The rustle might have been a tiger, in which case the fight-or-flight mechanism would have been useful – a person needed to begin to run before they saw a face appear and recognized it as a man-eating tiger. On the other hand the rustle might have been just a breeze rippling through the grass. In that case the person would have sprinted to 'safety' and found themselves standing breathless, with a pounding heart and sweating palms without having had any real cause to be afraid.

2 All these hundreds of thousands of years later, humans still react to perceived threats with the short route in the brain. Now, as then, humans react to threats *without thinking*.

Reacting without thinking

Have you ever been lying comfortably dozing in bed at night and heard a sudden bang or creak? If so, how did you react? It's most likely that you will have frozen still with your heart beating fast before you'd had any time to work out what caused the noise. Or, while you've been driving a car or riding a bike, have you ever seen a shadow move from out of the corner of your eye and swerved or made a very quick emergency stop before you could make out what the shadow was? Have you ever been engrossed in a task and jumped with a gasp at the lightest touch of someone's hand on your shoulder?

CASE STUDY

I can remember a time when I was asleep in my ground-floor bedroom. It was summer and I had the window open to let in some cool night air. I awoke suddenly to the sensation of something warm and furry wrapped around my neck. In a split second I was up and out of bed with heart pounding and palms sweating, and the neighbour's poor cat cowering in the corner where I had thrown it! Of course, if my brain had taken the time to work out that this was just the neighbour's cat I would have said hello and given it a stroke. But, my brain's short route had kicked in and made me react in less than a second, without thinking, to a 'perceived' threat that wasn't really a threat at all.

You might like to be reassured that the cat suffered no ill–effects and we have made friends again.

The short route in the brain is at work in all of these examples. It is the 'un-thinking' survival response; the unconscious fear response. This is the true *stress response*. People need it. It is vital for all those kinds of situations where, even though a bump in the night might just be a door pushed shut by a breeze, it might also be an intruder. Even though a shadow moving in the road might be just the waving branches of a tree, it might also be a child suddenly rushing out into the road. People need the short route in the brain so they can react instantly when their own or someone else's survival is at stake.

But how often do people find themselves in this kind of situation these days? Unless your work or hobbies take you into encounters with other people or situations that are inherently potentially dangerous, it is really very rare for your life to even seem to be threatened, let alone for you to be in actual danger.

Yet your short brain route fires time and time again *every day*, raising your stress levels. Why? Our definition of stress told you.

What is it that triggers your short route every day as you live your relatively safe life in today's modern environment? Write it here:

> The trigger for the short route in modern everyday life is...

Again, the answer is on the next page.

The trigger for the short route in modern everyday life is the perception of being unable to cope.

When we explored our definition of stress we said that the perception of being unable to cope triggers fear. We said:

As far as your instinct for survival is concerned, being unable to cope is as much a threat to your life as a physical attack would be, and that instinct for survival reacts in the same way to both – with the fight-or-flight response.

Now you can understand how and why that happens. The amygdala is not a 'thinking' part of the brain. So:

1 It can't tell the difference between a psychological threat (perceiving that you can't cope) and a physical threat (a noise in your house at night).

and

2 It reacts to both of these kinds of threat so quickly that it triggers the fight-or-flight response before the brain can register whether what's happening is a real threat or not.

It doesn't wait for the thinking brain to work out whether you really can cope or not, or whether the noise is really an intruder or not. It doesn't think; it just reacts. This is the true stress response.

Taking control of the stress response

We've taken a long time to explain the way the stress response happens in the brain. That's because you need to understand this if you are going to be able to manage your own stress levels more effectively.

You need to know that, as part of the brain's short route, the amygdala is responsible for triggering your instinctive fight-or-flight mechanism. You need to understand that the amygdala developed millions of years before the pre-frontal cortex. It is an ancient and primitive part of the brain. Humans share that part of the brain with all other creatures on earth that have a brain. All such creatures respond to perceived and real threats to survival by the short route via the amygdala.

The difference between humans and all those other animals is that humans have an incredibly highly developed pre-frontal cortex. This is the 'thinking brain'. This thinking brain gives you the ability to reflect on things, and to compare and analyse. Unlike those other animals, you can calculate, plan and make decisions. Yet, like them, your emotions and behaviour are very often dictated by a primitive part of your brain that can't think.

It is absolutely necessary and appropriate for this part of your brain to dictate your emotions and behaviour in the face of physical threats. That's what it is for. You need to react very quickly to a potential threat like a noise in the house at night or a shadow moving across the road as these are just the modern-day equivalent of man-eating tigers. Even if it turns out that what you were reacting to wasn't a real threat at all, your ability to react in less than a second might have saved your life, or that of someone else. These kinds of trigger for the fight-or-flight response happen quite rarely and your body is well adapted to recover from this kind of infrequent acute stress.

But, we do want to explore how you can manage your fear response to the psychological threat of your perception of being unable to cope. This kind of fear is not triggered rarely and acutely. It is triggered constantly and chronically every day by the challenges of work, family, finance, travel, etc. It is not appropriate for the primitive, non-thinking part of your brain to dictate your responses to these complex 21st-century experiences and events, and your body is not well adapted to handle this kind of continual stress (the next chapter will look at the many ways that chronic stress can affect a person's mental and physical well-being and undermine resilience).

For complex modern-day challenges you need to be able to allow yourself the extra couple of seconds it takes to use your brain's long route and *think*. You can't stop the short route firing when it perceives a psychological threat in a particular situation. That is instinctive and unconscious, and you can't control something that is outside of your conscious awareness. What you can do is gradually teach your brain what is and what isn't worth being afraid of until the short route begins to fire less and less often. That takes time and reasoning, and this is what the long route is for. Our 7 KEYS will show you how to use that long route to handle life's challenges in more mindful, appropriate and constructive ways.

The effects of modern-day chronic stress (and how those effects undermine resilience)

03

As we said earlier, since the stress response happens at an instinctive and unconscious level, sometimes the only way you will know you are experiencing stress is through the signs and symptoms that you can see and feel in your body. It is only then that you will realize something is happening within you that has the potential to put your well-being at risk and that you need to take action to stop it.

So it is very important for you to develop a good awareness of the possible signs and symptoms of stress. Stress reveals itself in different ways in different people. As well as having a general awareness you need to be able to recognize your own unique stress signs.

We'll explore the range of possible indications of stress here and then you can identify which ones relate to you personally.

We could just give you a long list to read. But we have found it is very easy to forget lists if you only glance over them. If you play a part in developing the resource yourself then you are much more likely to remember and become aware of your own signs and symptoms of stress when they arise.

It is highly likely that you have experienced the effects of stress at some time to some degree and that you will have noticed its effects on others too. Also, you may have read about stress in books or articles. Perhaps you have attended a stress-management course where you explored this topic. Use all of these sources of knowledge and experience to complete the exercise below.

Exercise one

Stress can affect all aspects of a person. It can affect their body (physical), how they feel (emotional), what they think about themselves and the world (psychological) and the things they do (behavioural). Some may say that it also affects people's spirituality. For this exercise we have used only the first four as headings. However, we wouldn't want to underestimate the damage that can be caused to a person's resilience by the loss of their sense of spirituality or spiritual beliefs through stress. So please do note this if you think it is important.

We'd like you to write down some signs and symptoms of stress under each of the headings in the table below. You'll probably find that there is some overlap between the different categories. For example, when people are stressed they sometimes become weepy – is that emotional or behavioural? Either would be correct, so don't worry too much about which column to put things, as that's not the main point of the exercise. The point is to enhance your awareness of the range of possible effects of stress, and how these have the potential to undermine a person's well-being.

We need 10 signs and symptoms in each column. We've provided a couple of examples to get you started. See if you can complete the table.

PHYSICAL	EMOTIONAL	PSYCHOLOGICAL	BEHAVIOURAL
What happens to the body when people are stressed? Think of signs that you can see on the outside of the body and those on the inside that you can't see.	*How do people feel when they're stressed?*	*What do people think about themselves, their lives and the world in general when they're stressed?*	*What do people do when they're stressed?*
headaches	weepy	I'm useless	overeating/eating too little
high blood pressure	anxious	I'm alone	nail biting

Reflect

What was it like to do that exercise? Was it easy, or difficult?

People who attend our courses always find it very easy to draw up long lists of signs and symptoms and we expect it was the same for you. Stress is so widespread that it would be very unusual to find a person who didn't know a fair amount about the problems that it causes, either through their own or other people's experience.

If you'd had more time and space, would you have been able to write down more examples?

In fact, there are a great deal more than 10 possible entries under each of the headings. Have a look at the completed table opposite.

PHYSICAL	EMOTIONAL	PSYCHOLOGICAL	BEHAVIOURAL
What happens to the body when people are stressed? Think of signs that you can see on the outside of the body and those on the inside that you can't see.	*How do people feel when they're stressed?*	*What do people think about themselves, their lives and the world in general when they're stressed?*	*What do people do when they're stressed?*
headaches	weepy	I'm useless	overeating/eating too little
high blood pressure	anxious	I'm alone	nail biting
Irritable Bowel Syndrome	irritable	everyone's against me	increased drug abuse – most commonly tobacco and alcohol
back pain	impatient	no one cares	crying
heart disease	depressed	if I ask for help they will think I'm weak/ incompetent/ a malingerer	argumentative
skin conditions, eg eczema	overwhelmed	I can't cope/ everyone else can cope so why can't I?	sleeplessness/ oversleeping
obesity/weight loss	nervous	the world is a terrible place	shouting and swearing
digestive problems	panicky	there's no light at the end of the tunnel	punching and kicking
ulcers	miserable	it's all my fault	withdrawal from social circle/family
frequent illnesses & infections	in despair	I'll never get over this	denial

This is a completed table, but it certainly is not the only possible correct table. You will probably have some of the same symptoms on your list, and also you will have thought of others that aren't on our list. This doesn't mean that some are right and some are wrong. If your list contains signs and symptoms that you are genuinely aware of through your own experience, observation and research, then they will be right even if they don't appear on ours.

All of the entries from your table and our table put together illustrate the extent of the potential damage that stress can cause to an individual person's body and mind, and to their ability to enjoy life and recover from setbacks quickly and effectively.

How stress undermines resilience

As you've seen, stress is the 'fight-or-flight response'. It is the body's immediate reaction when it receives short-route messages from the brain that tell it there is a threat to that body's survival. You almost certainly knew the phrase 'fight-or-flight' before you picked up this book. You will also be very familiar with what it feels like; racing heart, sweaty palms and 'butterflies' in your stomach. Then, once the threat is removed and you feel safe again, your heart rate returns to normal, your palms cool and dry, and your stomach settles down.

But, how does a natural survival mechanism that begins in the brain lead to such a range of symptoms that so greatly undermine a body's health and a person's sense of well-being and resilience? And why do these symptoms often become chronic (long-lasting and often worsening) when the immediate signs are so fleeting?

The reason is that this incredibly quick process in the brain (remember, just a tenth of a second) sets off a complex chain of hormonal and chemical reactions in the body. These chemical and hormonal reactions have powerful effects on the organs of the body.

When the brain perceives a threat it sends an 'alert' message via the nervous system to the adrenal glands in the body and they begin to pour out adrenalin. The chemical noradrenalin, which also gears the body up for fight-or-flight, is released at the same time throughout the nervous system. The physical symptoms of racing heart, cold clammy skin and butterflies in the stomach arise directly out of the physiological changes that happen when adrenalin and noradrenalin flow into the body:

- heart rate goes up to speed delivery of oxygen and glucose to muscles that you use to fight or to run – breathing becomes quicker and shallower too for this reason;

- blood is diverted from the skin and digestive system to muscles – this has the effect of making your skin feel cold and clammy, and is the cause of the fluttering sensation in the stomach.

It is true that the body tends to return to normal functioning quite quickly once the threat is removed, and there will be no long-term damage if this process takes place only rarely. However, we're sure you can see that if the process is repeated over and over again in response to situations that arise in everyday life then the body is likely to be more seriously harmed. Chronically raised heart rate can lead to abnormal heart rhythm or even affect the heart muscle itself. Continual lack of blood supply to the skin and digestive system can lead to problem-skin conditions and digestive disturbances.

These are just the effects that you are able to be aware of. Adrenalin and noradrenalin also affect blood pressure and the amount of insulin released into the blood stream. Again, this is not harmful if it happens for rare brief moments. But when these effects are repeated frequently over a long period of time then the body's natural functions can begin to be seriously undermined.

Another reason for the range and chronic nature of stress symptoms is that, as well as the release of adrenalin and noradrenalin, there is a second wave of response to a perceived threat, which involves the release of cortisol. Cortisol is released in the body as part of the body's normal cycle (known as the 'circadian rhythm'). Levels of cortisol are highest in the morning and lowest in the evening. However, cortisol is released in great quantities during the fight-or-flight response. For this reason it is often called the 'stress hormone'.

Like adrenalin and noradrenalin, cortisol has a powerful effect on the body's functions. That's because it:

- breaks down stored carbohydrates, fats and proteins to increase the level of glucose in the blood;
- lowers the amount of glucose taken up by the body tissues;
- increases the amount of glucose taken up by the brain;
- stimulates the breakdown of proteins into amino acids;
- regulates the cardiovascular system to maintain high blood pressure;
- is an immunosuppressant.

All these actions are extremely useful when facing a threat. A threatened animal can't stop to eat but needs energy, especially in the brain so it can take in a lot of information very quickly. So lots of stored glucose is released into the blood and taken up by the brain. Increased levels of amino acids enable quicker repair of tissue damage. For unknown reasons an immediate effect of stress (adrenalin) is to cause certain arteries to dilate. This means they widen. As a result, blood pressure is lowered. Cortisol counteracts this to bring blood pressure back up to normal. The immunosuppressant effect of cortisol controls inflammation and other immune processes that would hamper the body in its immediate need to be very active – you certainly do not need to start feeling ill or to have injured tissues or joints swelling up while you are trying to fight off or run away from an attack.

So, just like adrenalin and noradrenalin, cortisol is not a 'bad' or 'dangerous' hormone in itself. In normal circumstances it has a vital part to play in maintaining the balance of the body's functions. In situations of danger it manages those functions to help the body to act most effectively.

BUT, frequent stress reactions lead to constantly raised high levels of cortisol and this is damaging to health in the longer term. It can lead to hypertension (chronic high blood pressure). Hypertension is a major risk factor for heart attack and congestive heart failure, and is the most important risk factor for stroke. Raised levels of fatty acids can increase cholesterol levels. Also, because cortisol is an immunosuppressant, abnormally high levels can lead to a marked decrease in the body's ability to fight infection and disease.

External threats have been replaced by internal threats

The point is that the stress response is well designed for survival against external threats that happen only from time to time and can be fought off or escaped quickly, as was the case for our ancient ancestors. Those kinds of external threats are thankfully very rare for most people these days. However, external threats have been replaced by *internal* threats. These internal threats are people's perceptions, specifically their perceptions of being unable to cope with the day-to-day challenges of modern society.

We've described how people's primitive and instinctive fight-or-flight reaction is triggered by these internal threats. But, how do you fight off or run away from a perception? A perception has the power to threaten you every moment of the day, time and time again, and there is no physical way to fight or escape. Sure, you can do things that resemble a 'fight' like having a tough workout in a gym or using a punch bag. You can do things that are like 'flight' such as going for a run. These kinds of activities are useful up to a point. They help the body to disperse some of the chemical build-up, which is why you feel calmer immediately afterwards. But the perceptions are still there and able to set off the stress response again at any time, causing those chemicals and hormones to be released into your body over and over again. That is why symptoms of stress have become so chronic and harmful these days, and why they have such an ability to undermine a person's resilience.

But, don't despair. There are ways that you can deal with these perceptions without the need either to fight or to flee.

You know now that your stress reaction is triggered initially via the brain's short route. In that first fraction of a second you are not even aware it is happening so you can't stop it. But then, after a couple more seconds, you can become very conscious that you are experiencing stress and why. At that point you can tackle it. Not physically, but with your mind.

Managing stress to build resilience

04

So far we have been exploring the nature of resilience and stress, and we've described what we see as the relationship between the two. Now that you have this background knowledge and understanding we can begin to work on the main purpose of this book, which is to show you how you can manage stress and so build your resilience. Our strategies are contained in the 7 KEYS and you'll get to those soon in Part Two of this book. However, there is still some very important information that you need to be able to put those strategies into practice and reduce your stress effectively.

This information is in three key areas:

1 The signs and symptoms of stress.
2 The causes of stress.
3 Strategies and techniques to reduce stress.

1. The signs and symptoms of stress

We've explained that to have resilience means that you are able to return to your original, or an even stronger, mental and physical state following difficulty. Stress can undermine your ability to recover from the impact of life's challenges, and the inability to recover may lead to even further stress. It's the vicious circle we talked about. Remember this?

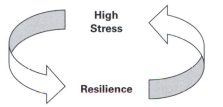

As you have seen from the range and potential seriousness of the symptoms of stress, it is very much worth avoiding this circle.

It is important to know the possible signs of stress because if you can be aware that you are experiencing stress at an early stage it is much easier to manage than it would be later when the symptoms are more severe. So keep in mind the signs and symptoms that you wrote down in Exercise One, along with those that we suggested. Take a few moments every now and again to become aware of your physical, mental and emotional states and to monitor your behaviour.

It is important to note that none of the signs and symptoms on your list and ours is necessarily an indication of stress. It doesn't necessarily mean that you are stressed if you get angry or have a good cry from time to time. By the same token, it doesn't mean you are suffering with stress just because you've come out in a skin-rash, or get headaches, or have an upset stomach, or even have high blood pressure. Some conditions are simply part of a person's genetic make-up. Or, they might be signs of natural reactions to temporary emotional upset or physical illness. Stress usually gives rise to a number of signs across the range of emotional, physical, behavioural and psychological symptoms. So if you have a physical symptom but don't feel particularly upset emotionally, the chances are that these are symptoms of a physical problem and you might need to get medical advice.

As a general rule, you should be alerted to stress if you notice a *change* in your normal state or behaviour that persists over a period of time, say a fortnight or so. People who are suffering with stress often say things like, 'That just wasn't like me!' or, 'I don't recognize myself any more.'

Even people who believe themselves to be very resilient should be watchful of this. Relatively minor experiences of stress can begin to chip away at that resilience leading to greater vulnerability to stress in the future.

Sometimes other people who know you well will be able to spot the signs more quickly than you could yourself. In this case it may be your colleague, friend or partner who says, 'That wasn't like you' or 'I just don't recognize you anymore'. Listen to them. Pay attention even though you might not want to hear it. Once you have worked through this book you will have all the knowledge you need to deal with it, so there is no need to fear or avoid the issue.

2. The causes of stress

It is important to be aware of the possible causes of stress because if you are able to identify the cause of your stress then you have the potential to remove that cause and so remove the stress.

When you know what is causing you to be stressed there are two, and *only ever two*, directions you can take:

i. Act on the world

Sometimes it is possible to act on the outside world to remove the cause of your stress. If so you should do that as soon and as quickly as you can. For example, you may be aware that you are becoming stressed because your computer keeps crashing. In that case it might be a simple matter of getting your computer fixed or replacing it. Or, if you are stressed because you are struggling with too much work or too many personal commitments it may be possible to drop some of that or get help. If someone else's behaviour is leading you to feel stressed you can point this out to them and ask them to behave differently.

Of course, it isn't always easy to act on the world in these ways. That's because there is very often an element of risk. If you can't afford to repair or replace your computer then to do so could be a financial risk. It might be risky on a personal level to approach people for help or to ask them to behave differently towards you. They may not be keen to help you reduce your workload or personal commitments if they benefit from your efforts. They may be angry or hurt if they feel criticized by you. So you could risk the loss of ease in a relationship, or even of the relationship itself.

Even though there is always the potential for loss or pain if you take action, sometimes there is a greater risk to your health, relationships, job, etc if you do not. At those times you must act to protect yourself, and possibly others from the risks of stress.

Ultimately, this might involve a decision on your part to leave a job or a relationship, or whatever is causing you stress. This might seem negative and like a kind of surrender. In fact it is just another way of acting on the world to remove a stressor. And, of course, people do that sometimes. They do walk away from jobs that they can no longer tolerate, and they do end relationships that have become too painful or damaging. You yourself have probably done something like that at some time in your life.

Whether your choice to act on the world involves simply starting a difficult conversation with someone or making a life-changing decision, you need a particular set of skills and qualities to enable you to take action even when this is a real challenge. One of our aims in this book is to show you what these skills and qualities are and guide you towards developing those.

ii. Act on yourself

We've explained how sometimes it can be very hard to change the external world and get rid of the cause of your stress. In some situations you may even feel that it is impossible.

For example, you may tell a friend, colleague or family member that their behaviour is causing you to become stressed. They may not acknowledge that or agree to change. It is difficult to stay but you feel that it would be much more painful to leave. Or, you may work in an environment where pressure is inevitably high, either because of the nature of the job or because of a staff shortage, etc. In that case it may be unrealistic to expect to be able to reduce your own workload, but you feel that the risk to your financial security would be too great to bear if you left the job.

Does that mean that there is no way to escape the stress in these situations? We would say that the way to deal with stress in these cases is to act on *yourself*.

You need to find a way to remove the cause of your stress by reacting differently *at a deep psychological level* to the person or situation. Once you do that you will respond in a way that is protective of your well-being however difficult the circumstances might be.

Since the things that cause people to become stressed are so frequently outside of their power to change, this ability to work on your own reactions and behaviour is crucial to protect you from raised stress levels and potential damage to your resilience.

NB – there is no number three!

There are only these two ways to make sure that the events and situations that arise in your life do not damage you; act on the world, or act on yourself. And, there is only one person who has the power to take one or other of those directions. That person is you.

This doesn't mean that other people have no responsibility at all to behave in ways that protect your mental and physical well-being. They do have some responsibility for that, and so do you towards them. At work, employers have a legal 'duty of care' towards their employees. As an employee you have a duty to comply with your employer's efforts to protect you. In your personal life, you and your friends, family and partners have a responsibility towards each other that comes from an emotional commitment or familial bond.

However, sometimes people neglect their duty of care (whether deliberately or not) and when they do it will be up to you to take care of yourself. Again, this book and our 7 KEYS will show you how.

But, what if you don't know what's causing your stress?

The two directions described above – to act on the world and to act on yourself – apply when you are able to identify the cause or causes of your stress. But there may be times when you realize you're suffering from some of the symptoms of stress and can't quite put your finger on why this is happening.

If there is no major difficulty or upset in your life, it might be that your stress is being triggered by the build up of a number of smaller events. You stub your toe getting out of bed, then you burn the toast, then you miss your train to work and the next train is cancelled. When you eventually get to work the computer system is down and your manager comes to you with yet another report to write by yesterday. You go out for lunch and find your wallet is missing. A signal failure means your train home is delayed – for the third time that week. At last you get home. You pour yourself the glass of red wine you've been looking forward to since you stubbed your toe getting out of bed that morning... and then you spill it all over your brand new cream-coloured carpet. What do you do? You can probably imagine this scenario quite vividly. You might shout and swear, kick the furniture and slam the door, or you might go completely silent and mop tearfully at the mess – all of which are signs of stress.

If the rest of your day had been pleasant and relaxing it is unlikely that the spilt wine on its own would be enough to cause these extreme reactions; the wine on the carpet would not, in itself, be the cause of your stress. So what would have reduced you to shouting and tears? Was it the stubbing of your toe? The train delays? The computer failure? The manager asking for more work? The answer is yes, yes, yes and yes.

A number of small events building up on each other over time can lead to stress just as powerfully as a single, big life event. You will be able to use what you learn from this book to build a solid base of internal resilience that will ensure these relatively minor daily setbacks and irritations don't lead to the damaging effects of stress.

3. Strategies and techniques to reduce stress

Earlier, we talked a little about the different types of strategies and techniques that people use to combat stress. There we suggested that many traditional methods of stress management such as deep-breathing exercises, calming music and massage tend to lower anxiety and reduce the effects of stress only in the short term.

Here's a simple example. Let's say you are becoming stressed by a relationship at work. During the day you have upsetting encounters with that person. Even when you are not actually with them you feel anxious and unhappy if you know they are around. From time to time you go off on your own to take some deep breaths and count slowly to 10. This calms you down so that you can get on with your tasks for the day. When you get home you put some relaxing music on and stroke the dog or cat for a while until you feel better. Then you go back to work the next day and, guess what? That person is still there and you become just as anxious and unhappy as before.

As we said earlier, we would describe the approach of finding a soothing escape from immediate feelings of anxiety as 'damage limitation' rather than stress management. That's because it does just that – it limits the damage caused by your stress. And that is a valuable and important thing to do because it helps you to maintain a certain level of well-being. However, we believe that unless you take action to do something about the causes of stress themselves – either by acting on the world or acting on yourself at a psychological level – this precious sense of well-being will be gradually chipped away and it will only be a matter of time before the stress symptoms become too severe to limit or disguise.

To manage your stress in a way that is truly effective you need to act in a way that will have a much more profound effect on your life and on yourself as a person. You will understand more what this means as you continue with the work in this book.

What you already know (and why what you know isn't helping you)

In the last chapter we identified three key areas that you need to know about to be able to manage your stress effectively. They were the signs and symptoms of stress, the causes of stress and strategies to reduce stress. We are going to explore these in more detail now to make sure that you have all the information that you need.

In fact, we have already done this with the signs and symptoms of stress in Exercise One. We hope you now have sufficient knowledge and awareness of those to be able to recognize your own personal signs of stress and when you need to take action to manage and reduce that stress. We hope too that our descriptions and explanations of the very real and lasting damage that can be done by stress will motivate you to take action quickly and courageously when you need to.

Now we will move on to the other two areas: the causes of stress and the strategies and techniques for managing it.

As we did with the signs and symptoms, we would like to know what you already know about causes and strategies before we present our own ideas.

Exercise two

1. Causes of stress

In the box below, write down 10 aspects of life (from any area of life – home, family, social, work) that you believe could lead a person to become stressed. What are the kinds of events or experiences that people find difficult to manage? People in our face-to-face groups often identify things like work deadlines, traffic jams, debt, moving house, etc. Can you think of 10 more?

What causes stress & undermines resilience?

1

2

3

4

5

6

7

8

9

10

2. Strategies to reduce stress

Now, in the next box write down 10 things that people do to reduce their stress and build their resilience. What are the techniques you yourself use to relieve your stress? What techniques have you heard about from others or read about in books and magazines, etc? Here, people often identify practices such as exercise, aromatherapy, reading, listening to music, etc. Can you think of 10 more?

Techniques and strategies to reduce stress & build resilience

1

2

3

4

5

6

7

8

9

10

Reflect

What was it like for you to do that exercise?

People in our groups most often find this exercise quite easy and they usually produce many more than 10 items under each heading. We expect you could have written more if you'd had more time and space.

When people work together in groups they find they agree on the kinds of things they want to include. Regardless of where they live, their personal background, age, gender, type and level of job etc, people seem to find the same kinds of situations and events stressful, and they believe the same kinds of actions and activities will be helpful in reducing their stress.

We've created the lists below from samples of our groups' responses. Take a look at these and see how much they reflect your own thoughts.

1. What causes stress and undermines resilience?

(We didn't ask you to put your items under category headings such as 'Work' and 'Family', but we've done that here for clarity.)

Work:

too much or too little

balancing work and life

insecurity, threat of redundancy

relationships with managers and colleagues

under-resourcing

lack of control

having to do things you don't like or aren't good at

conflicting demands

frequent change

lack of communication

bullying

other people's expectations

Relationships outside of work:

beginnings and endings

communication

other people's expectations

Family:

divorce

conflicting needs of different family members

disagreements and arguments

coping with illness, disability, etc

Home:

moving house

home maintenance

difficult neighbours

Children:

safety

education

noise

messiness

discipline

lack of control

The environment and where you live:

space

lack of control

noise

safety

appearance

Personal:

poor health or injury

ageing

bereavement

general financial worries and debt

commuting – traffic and public transport

holidays

2. Techniques and strategies to reduce stress and build resilience

manage your time

prioritize

say 'no'

delegate

get a better work–life balance

have a more positive attitude (glass half full instead of half empty)

take breaks in the working day

take holidays

me-time

exercise

go to relaxation classes

be assertive

watch TV

listen to music

aromatherapy massage

aromatherapy baths

walking in the countryside

talk to someone

ask for help

do breathing exercises

yoga

dig the garden

let off steam

Are the items on your lists reflected in these two sections? Would you agree with items that do not appear in your lists? As we've said, we have found a great deal of agreement and shared experience in our groups. So we're pretty sure that your answer to these questions will be 'yes' or 'mostly'. If you wrote down ideas that don't appear on these lists, other people would probably agree with those too.

It would appear from these exercises that you already seem to know all you need to know to be able to manage your stress levels effectively. You know what aspects of life can cause you to feel stressed and undermine your ability to be resilient. You know what kinds of physical, emotional and behavioural signs to look out for. You even know what to do if you start to suffer from stress and find your resilience failing. You know all of this from your own personal experience, and from the experiences of others around you. You may also have gathered information and advice though books, media, counselling services, support networks, etc.

So, here's a question. What do you need this book for?

It's because even though you have all this knowledge... you're still stressed!

You are not alone in this. All the groups we meet can do the exercises above without much difficulty and yet many tell us that they are 'very stressed'.

So it seems that even though people's knowledge about stress is growing, the problem of stress is increasing. It doesn't add up. How can that be?

Why what you know about stress isn't helping you

We find it useful to compare the problem of stress with that of being over-weight. It might seem a strange approach but bear with us.

Imagine that this book was about how to lose weight. Imagine that we asked you to write down what causes a person to become overweight and the techniques and strategies for losing weight. Would you be able to do that? Of course you would.

Medical conditions aside, there are two things that people need to do to lose weight. Write them down here in big, bold capital letters before you read on:

To lose weight people need to...

1

2

Gold stars if you said something along the lines of 'EAT FEWER CALORIES' and 'DO MORE EXERCISE'. Everyone knows this by now, don't they? There is an industry worth billions that says it through huge numbers and varieties of books, CDs, DVDs, support groups and clubs, etc. These all tell people in many different ways... exactly the same thing. The solution to weight gain is never ice-cream and sofa; it is always broccoli and gym. Eat less and move around more. It isn't a complicated solution. So why is it still such a struggle for most people who want to lose weight? It isn't that they don't know how.

We believe that if people fail to beat either weight gain or stress it is because they have not been looking at the *real causes* of their difficulty. If you don't look at the real causes you will not find solutions that really work.

For example, if you see 'eating too much and exercising too little' as the cause of weight gain then the solution is to eat less and exercise more. That makes perfect sense of course. Except that it doesn't work because 'eating too much and exercising too little' is very rarely the real cause. To discover the real cause you need to ask 'WHY?' You need to ask:

> WHY does a person eat too much and exercise too little when they know they need to do the exact opposite to lose weight?

There are many possible answers to this question. It might be because they are reacting to trauma, or neglect, or loneliness, or damaged self-esteem, or loss, or emotional 'emptiness' – or a whole range of possible *underlying psychological issues*. Perhaps being overweight has become part of their identity and they are afraid of what will happen to that identity if they become slim. Maybe they are afraid of how other people will react to their new image. Perhaps they feel they need to hide behind their large size. It may just be that they lack motivation because they find eating too pleasurable and the sofa too comfortable! All these examples reflect the real causes of overweight. These are the deep psychological causes. If you look at it like this, then overeating and lack of exercise are not the causes; they're actually the symptoms of something going on at a deeper level.

If you tackle a problem by working on the symptoms you will not find a solution that is effective in the long term. People will always struggle to lose weight unless they take steps to address the underlying psychological causes of their weight problem.

CASE STUDY

This book is not about losing weight, but here's a little advice if you are trying to do that. The advice is: stop asking '*How* can I lose weight?' You already know the answer to that question. To succeed you need to discover the underlying cause of your problem. You do that by asking '*Why*'; 'Why am I eating ice-cream and sitting on the sofa when I know I need to eat broccoli and go to the gym?' When you have the answer to that question and can start to deal with the real issue, then you'll be able to achieve your goal of losing weight effectively and long term. How? By doing what you already know you need to do; by changing your diet and doing more exercise.

It's the same with stress.

The reason that what you know about stress isn't helping you is that you are not addressing the real underlying causes of your stress. If you want to succeed in beating stress then first you have to discover what these are. To do that you have to stop asking 'How can I manage my stress better?' You already know the answer to that. Now you need to start asking 'Why...?'

You need to ask questions like:

'Why do I say "yes" to things I don't have time to do when I know I need to manage my time and *say "no"*?'

'Why do I say "yes" to things I don't want to do when I know I need to *set my own priorities*?'

'Why do I wear myself out by trying to do everything when I know I need to *delegate work* or *ask people to do their share* of the tasks at home?'

'Why do I struggle silently to handle an impossible workload when I know I need to *let my manager know I'm unable to cope and get help*?'

'Why do I get more and more worked up if I'm stuck in a traffic jam or my train is delayed when I know I need to *take some deep breaths* to stay calm?'

... and so on.

Once you have the answers to those questions you will know the deep underlying psychological causes of your stress. When you can start to deal with these issues, then you will be able to manage your stress really effectively and build deep and long-lasting resilience that will see you through the toughest times.

How?

By doing the things that you already know – by saying 'no' and managing your time, by delegating and asking people to do their share, by setting your own priorities, by being honest when you need help, by taking deep breaths and calming down, and all of the other great strategies that you already know about.

CASE STUDY

At a stress-management training day for a group of head teachers, there was a person at the session so stressed that she could barely speak. Each time she tried to say something she broke down in tears. Her deputy revealed that this head teacher had not taken her holidays for a long time. So we asked the head teacher, 'How useful would it be if we said you need to take your holidays to feel less stressed?' She just shook her head. No, it would not be useful. Why? Because she already knew that. She knew how she could manage her stress. What she didn't know was why she wasn't doing what she knew she needed to do. Once she understood why she wasn't taking her holidays, and could deal with that issue, then she would be able to manage her stress – by taking her holidays.

Only two real causes of stress

We believe there are only two underlying psychological causes of stress, and will present those to you soon in our KEY 1. However, we'd like you to see if you can work out what they are for yourself before we do that.

Exercise three

Take a look again at those WHY questions that we suggested you ask in relation to managing stress. Ask yourself:

'Why do people say "yes" to things they don't have time to do when they know they need to manage their time and *say "no"*?'

'Why do people say "yes" to things they don't want to do when they know they need to *set their own priorities*?'

'Why do people wear themselves out by trying to do everything when they know they need to *delegate work* or *ask people to do their share* of the tasks at home?'

Also, take another look at the story of the stressed-out head teacher who didn't take her holidays. Why do you think she was not taking breaks when she needed to?

We believe that for each of these questions there are only *two* possible answers. This means we believe there are only *two* underlying psychological causes of stress (unlike weight gain where we suggested many different possible underlying psychological causes).

Would you be able to suggest what those two answers (and therefore the two causes) might be? Here are some clues to help you:

1 For some of the 'Why' questions only one of the two answers might apply, for some of them both answers might be appropriate.

2 Think about each of the 'Why' questions in terms of:

   a how people are affected by what others think and feel about them (and what they want others to think and feel about them).

and

   b the amount of influence people have over events or situations that arise in their lives (and the amount of influence they want to have).

3 It might help if your answers start like this:

'Because people need...'

4 If you're still struggling, take a look at the list of causes of stress that we provided earlier from groups that we've worked with before. You'll find both of the two underlying psychological causes in this list.

Write down your answers here:

1   **2**

PART TWO
The 7 KEYS

KEY 1

> **Let go of your need to be liked and in control**
>
> *Needing to be liked by everyone and in control of everything drains your energy. Be disliked sometimes. Be less than perfect. It's your life.*

The two underlying psychological causes of stress

1. The need for approval

In Exercise Three we asked you to see if you could work out what our two underlying psychological causes of stress might be. For one of these you would have been on the right lines if you put down anything that relates to people's need to live up to the expectations of others, and their need for others to have a good opinion of them. In a nutshell, people need other people to like them. And, they spend a lot of their time and energy doing things that they believe will achieve this.

Please note that approval is very different from respect. It is possible for other people to respect you without liking you. In fact, if you do things that could earn you respect, it often comes at the expense of approval. For example, people might not like you if you say 'no' to them, but they might very well respect you. You say 'yes' because it's their approval you seek.

Why is the need for approval such a powerful psychological driver?

i. Infant development

One reason may be that it is very likely to be rooted in childhood. In infancy you needed to keep adult carers physically close to you so they could provide you with food and shelter. More than this, you needed to ensure a level of attraction that would bring a certain amount of physical affection such as stroking, hugging and kissing. These are just as crucial to survival as food and shelter.

Psychologists have compared the development of babies cared for by a loving mother with those who had been looked after in orphanages in countries affected by conflict. All of the babies were cared for in hygienic surroundings and had good food and medical care. However, there was one major difference. The babies who were cared for by their mothers were held, kissed and stroked. Those in orphanages received very little, or even none, of that kind of treatment. Their carers simply did not have the time or resources to give each child such intense one-to-one loving attention. In the orphanages 34 out of 91 babies died before their second year. The development of babies who survived was severely limited. Most couldn't speak, they couldn't eat alone and they were all incontinent. It is clear that food and shelter alone are not sufficient for children's survival. They also need love.

So, as a baby, you needed to be loveable in order to survive. You didn't know this in a conscious way of course. As a newborn you used certain behaviours instinctively to bring adult carers close to you. You screamed and cried, and adults would come running. They'd pick you up, coo at you, and kiss and stroke you as well as feeding you. Then they began to become tired and impatient with your screaming and crying. They started to say to each other 'You go, it's your turn!' As they fed you there would be less of the gentle cooing, kissing and stroking because they just wanted to get the feeding over with quickly. At this point you developed a new behaviour. You began to smile.

Now, we don't know for certain what brings about a baby's first smile. Some say it is just an accident, or imitation, or wind. But whatever brought about that first smile, the reason you kept doing it was because it had the most extraordinary effect on the people around you. Instead of being annoyed and trying to avoid contact with you, everyone wanted to gather round and see this cute, smiling baby. Suddenly everyone wanted to hold you and kiss you. They started to coo at you again (cooing is an essential part of a baby's development of language and communication – remember those orphans who couldn't speak...).

From the very earliest weeks and months of your life, your brain was making a powerful connection between smiling and gaining a lot of the things that you needed in order to survive. A pattern was laid down and powerfully reinforced. That pattern was, 'Be as others want you to be and you will survive. Be contrary to how others want you to be and you will die.'

Of course that was true when you were an infant. If you had been abandoned, neglected or abused you could quite possibly have died. However, as an adult it is no longer necessarily true. Yet, you're still smiling to survive.

ii. Evolution

As well as the patterns learned in infancy, the power of the need to be liked might also have an evolutionary foundation. If you think about how people would have lived thousands of years ago, perhaps as nomadic tribes, any individual who was cast out from the tribe would have had a much lower chance of survival. People needed protection by the group against the very real physical threats they would have faced at that time; threats such as exposure to the elements, predators, competing tribes, etc. Without the safety provided by others they would have been very vulnerable. So they would have done or said whatever was required to be liked and accepted by the group and avoid rejection. To recognize the truth of this, you might think of some of the frightening, humiliating, and sometimes even extremely dangerous and painful initiation ceremonies that people have endured throughout the ages.

In our modern society, real physical threats to people's survival are very rare. Even so, patterns of behaviour developed through evolution are so deeply ingrained that people in this day and age still carry a profound and unconscious 'belief' that they need acceptance and inclusion by another person or by a group in order to survive.

It is this profound and unconscious 'belief', along with the survival instinct and patterns of learning from early childhood, that leads people to constantly seek the approval of others.

This is what leads people to say 'yes' when they need and want to say 'no'. It is what leads people to do things to fit in with other people's desires, demands and needs even when these go against their own desires and needs, and sometimes even against their own personal values. It is because of this that people are so driven to make everyone else happy that they would rather become ill with stress than state their own needs and values, and balance those with the demands of others.

A question answered

We have already discovered that you know how to manage stress. You know you need to manage your time, to achieve a balance between work and outside life, and between the conflicting needs of different family members. You know you need to make sure you have the time and space to do things you enjoy and that enable you to fulfil your own desires and ambitions.

You know you need to take a break to listen to music, or read, or dance, or meet friends, or even just do nothing for a while.

The question we asked was:

Why is it so difficult to do those things?

The answer is:

Because all of them require you to say 'no' sometimes to some people.

They require you, sometimes, to say what you need or prefer and to stand up for your own values.

They require you to state clearly what you want or intend to do even if this goes against what someone else wants or needs you to do.

But, if you say 'no' to someone, or assert your own needs, then they might be upset with you and not like you. They might think ill of you. They might think you're selfish or mean or uncaring or unhelpful, and they might reject you. They might even tell others how selfish and mean and uncaring you are and they will reject you too. You can't bear that because at a deep unconscious level, at the level of your instinct, you perceive this as a threat to your survival.

Now, remember what happens when you perceive something as a potential threat to your survival? The fight-or-flight response is triggered in the body. That reaction is the true stress response we discussed earlier. It operates via the short route in the brain. This is the route that enables a person's body to release stress hormones and chemicals in fractions of a second so they can be ready to run or fight to survive in an instant.

Remember also that this route leaves out the pre-frontal cortex, which is the part of the brain that thinks, analyses and reasons. This part of the brain knows that you won't die if someone doesn't like you. It knows that you are a grown-up person with the means to take care of yourself. It knows that, while it might be unpleasant if you lose somebody's approval and acceptance, you will not die. This part of the brain knows that this perceived threat to your survival is not a tiger; it is really just the wind rustling the grass.

However, the thinking brain doesn't have time to tell you all of that in the fraction of the second it takes you to act out of fear.

So, before you have time to think it through, you will do something you'll regret later. You'll agree to something you'll wish you hadn't. You'll accept offensive behaviour that you'll wish you had challenged. You'll pay for a poor service or apologize for something when you have done nothing wrong. Without thinking, you'll be living a lifestyle according to what 'they' think you should do or have or desire, without regard to your own needs, views, and perhaps even your own deeply held values. We believe that living against your personal values is a very powerful source of stress and will be returning to this specific point later in this book.

For now we will focus on:

How the need to be liked affects stress levels in everyday life

It is this need for approval that makes it difficult and stressful to do things like maintaining boundaries, managing your time and workloads, achieving a balance between work and outside life that suits you personally, balancing needs of different family members and so on. Achieving balance will always mean saying 'no' to someone.

If you fulfil the needs of one family member then another will be disappointed.

If you invest a lot of time on your work then managers and colleagues will think well of you and approve, but family members will be dissatisfied and will disapprove. If you insist on leaving the office at a reasonable hour in order to spend some time with your family then your family will be happier and will approve, but managers and colleagues who stay later may become resentful and will disapprove.

Your family might be happy if you reduce your working hours even if this means a lower income, but your friends might be unhappy because you can no longer go out to expensive bars and restaurants with them.

Money issues can become a more general trigger for stress when you feel that you need to maintain a certain status or image that will lead others to think well of you. In our society and culture, status (which is achieved by gaining approval from others) is very tied up with financial success so it can be difficult to think about taking action that might threaten your financial position.

People's need for approval affects their behaviour in more general ways too. They might wear clothes that are uncomfortable or that they don't like in order to fit in with their group or 'tribe'. They might even engage in damaging or dangerous behaviour, such as drug-taking or risky sexual behaviour simply because they are afraid to say 'no'.

CASE STUDY

Think back to the stressed head teacher we talked about in Part One. It turned out she hadn't been taking her holidays. It was clear that she knew she should take some time off. What she didn't know was why she wasn't doing what she knew she needed to do. Part of the answer would be her need for approval. Overwork is often linked to the need for people to like you. But, while colleagues may think you're great and give you lots of approval while you keep taking on more and more, is that really worth the risk to your health? Also, stress doesn't only affect the sufferer. It affects their partners, children and friends too. It threatens their relationships, homes and jobs. Is it really worth taking such a risk just so that people will like you? Would it not be better and safer to take care of yourself and seek people's respect instead? Wouldn't it be better to recognize when enough is enough and say 'no'?

We're not saying it's ok to slack at work and say 'no' to something just because you don't feel like doing it. That would be unprofessional. We're saying be careful not to take on so much work that you become ill because you don't want to risk other people's criticism or disapproval.

It's the same outside work. We're not saying you should never do anything for other people. In fact there is a lot of research which shows that if you do something kind for someone else this lowers your stress and increases your feelings of happiness. In any case, there are people you want to help or spend time with and it would be uncaring and unfriendly not to do so. We're just saying be careful not to take on so many tasks or responsibilities at home or socially that you become exhausted and unwell.

People can find themselves struggling with another person's behaviour for a long time because they weren't able to challenge the person or say 'no' early on. Relationships between parents and their children are a classic example (give in to a child's screaming demands for sweets at a supermarket just once and see what happens...). But this is true between spouses, partners, friends and colleagues, too. Sometimes people go as far as to tolerate, and be damaged by, bullying and abuse in their relationships rather than challenge such behaviour immediately because they are afraid to risk rejection through being seen as a troublemaker. They are afraid to lose affection even from someone they fear or despise (they are more fearful of being cast out, or casting themselves out, from the tribe).

Even in the most difficult times, people are influenced by their need for other people's approval. Think about bereavement, for example. In bereavement people worry that they are grieving for 'too long' and they 'should be over it by now', or that they haven't grieved for 'long enough' and are laughing or going out 'too soon'.

Are these examples ringing bells with you? Take a few minutes to look back at your list of causes of stress in Part One. See if you can identify where these arise because of the need to be liked by others.

It seems that people need to be liked by *everyone*, even those they don't know, have never met before and will most likely never meet again. As a result they apologize to people who have walked into them. They pay hairdressers who have made a mess of a haircut and tell waiters in restaurants that everything is 'fine' when in fact their food is overcooked/undercooked/ not what they ordered. They are reluctant to take substandard goods back to a shop or complain about poor service because they don't want to be seen as difficult or unpleasant... by anyone. In their car, people feel anxious if another driver impatiently brings their car up very close behind them to indicate that they are going too slowly. They might even speed up a bit and drive faster than they would like so that someone they don't know and will never see again won't be angry or think less of them. The list could go on and on. How many of these do you recognize in yourself? Are there any other ways that you personally seek the approval of others who are really not important in your life?

> While you've been reading this section you might have thought, 'Hang on, this doesn't apply to me. I don't care what other people think!' Well, that may be true. If it is then you will be much less vulnerable to stress than others who do recognize that they are driven by this need. However, if you suffer from stress even though you don't need other people's approval it might be because you are more affected by the second underlying cause that we will explore shortly.
>
> Having said that, stop and ask yourself if it is really true that you don't need other people's approval, or are you just becoming defensive because it sounds like a weakness that you don't want to admit to?

Deeply ingrained patterns from evolution and childhood lead people to have an unconscious 'belief' that they need *everyone* to like them in order to survive. But, how many people do you actually need to like you?

Exercise four

Before you read on, write down here the people you actually need to approve of you; to like or love you. You will be able to identify these people by recognizing that your life would be very difficult or unpleasant if they didn't like you or if they removed their love or affection. Remember, this is about being liked and not about being respected.

Who would these people be:

At work?

....

....

....

....

At home?

....

....

....

....

Socially?

....

....

....

....

Reflect

These lists are usually very short indeed. People will often write down only one or two names in each of these areas of life. You might have written just 'myself' in one or more of the categories. It is great if that's true. It is the real meaning of 'self-esteem', and it is something that most people aspire to achieve. We would encourage this aspiration. We regard the ability to develop self-esteem as a cornerstone to building resilience. You will find that there is a lot more about this in the KEYS that follow so we won't expand on it here.

For now, you just need to be able to recognize that most people, probably including yourself, find it very difficult to maintain confidence in themselves without some signs that other people like them. In order to tackle stress effectively you need to be able to let go of your need for approval from everyone. Focus on the people who are really important in your life. Focus on the people whose approval or lack of it significantly affects your life.

And even then, remember that while you could find your life very difficult or painful if those people were to withdraw their approval, you would still survive.

When we present these ideas in our face-to-face courses people have the opportunity to ask questions and raise concerns. At this point these are generally about how to say 'no' and state their own needs, etc without becoming (or appearing) uncaring, difficult or unpleasant. If you have similar worries, we'd like to reassure you that we will present strategies and techniques to achieve this in a later KEY. For now you just need to think about whether or not you identify and agree with the explanation we've given in this part of KEY 1. As we said in our introductory section at the start of the book, ask yourself how the different ideas relate (or don't relate) to you and your own life, and be honest in your responses.

Is the need for approval a root cause of stress for you? If it is, you will soon discover how to let this go without undermining your own or anyone else's integrity.

The two underlying psychological causes of stress

2. The need for control

Think back again to Exercise Three where we asked you to see if you could work out what our two underlying psychological causes of stress might be. Well done if one of your ideas was something about control.

In fact, very often, 'lack of control' appears as an item in itself on lists of causes of stress along with things like bereavement, moving house, other people, traffic jams, workloads, etc. You might have written this as one of your causes in Exercise Two. But think about this for a moment. Why are bereavement, house move, other people, traffic jams, workloads, etc stressful? The reason is that each of these involves at least one element that is impossible for an individual to control. So 'lack of control' is not just a cause of stress like all the others. It is one of the two underlying psychological causes of stress.

For example, what is stressful about moving house? We would suggest that you are not stressed by the aspects of a house move that you can do, decide or manage. You are stressed by the things that you need other people to do, decide or manage. The mortgage, the legal issues, buyer's reliability, seller's reliability, the electricity, the gas, the telephone – all of this is out of your control because you cannot control other people. You can ask, beg, shout, threaten, demand, and that might work... or it might not. Ultimately, people will do what they will do and there is nothing that you can do about that.

So, we would say that a house move is not, in itself, a cause of stress. It is the need to be in control of things that are *not controllable* that is the cause of stress. The house move is just one of many situations and events that trigger stress which is actually caused by people's need for control.

Some people need to be in control of everything. These people will find a process like moving house very stressful. In fact, they will be vulnerable to stress generally because there are so many events and situations that occur in life that are out of people's control such as traffic jams, cancelled trains, family, the economy, the weather... and so on.

On the other hand, there are people who do not need to be in control of everything. These people are able to recognize that there are some elements of their lives that they can control, and some that they cannot. They do as much as they can to influence a situation, and then they let go. It isn't that they let go of the need to get things done. They continue to take actions and work towards achieving their aims. However, they let go of the worry and distress triggered by elements they cannot control, and this is a powerful skill in managing stress.

At this point in our workshops somebody usually says something like 'yes, but that's very hard to do!' We agree. It can be very difficult to let go if you are a person who tends to need to be in control. Like the need for approval, these patterns are laid down from early childhood and so they are very deeply ingrained. Also, like the need for approval, being in control could have been essential for survival thousands of years ago when the environment, predators and other groups of people were very real threats to an individual's life. Humans at that time would have needed to be able to accurately sense tiny changes in temperature, sound, smell and movement around them and use those signs to predict threats. They would have had to be able to take action, sometimes within fractions of a second, to make themselves and their tribe safe. That is the nature of control, and people still instinctively need to have that ability to keep all danger at bay.

The difficulty is, in our modern place and time where challenges are much more complex and constant, that simply is not possible.

The good news is that, most of the time nowadays, it doesn't matter that it is not possible for people to have that level of control. As we explained earlier, real physical threats to people's survival are very rare now. A delayed train or traffic jam might be inconvenient and have uncomfortable or challenging consequences; however, it will not kill you as a sabre-toothed tiger would if it was given a chance. Even so, as with the need for approval, evolutionary patterns are so deeply ingrained that people still carry a profound and unconscious 'belief' that they need to be in control of everything in order to survive.

It is because the need for control operates at this profound level of instinct that we say it is one of the two real causes of stress, along with the need for approval. We would say that all of the others you wrote down in Exercise Two are not real causes of stress. They are simply elements of your complex and demanding life that could cause you to become stressed, if you are not able (at least sometimes) to *let go*.

Let's have a look at the how the need for control and an inability to let go of that need can lead you to behave in ways that undermine your resilience and make you more vulnerable to the effects of stress. We can look at this under three broad headings.

Need for control – I

You need to be right

We'll begin to explore this idea with an exercise.

Exercise five

Take a moment to think about the last three arguments you've had with other people. Write down here who you argued with and what the arguments were about:

1 ....
....
....
....

2 ....
....
....
....

3 ....
....
....
....

Now go back to those notes and ask yourself for each of them:

Did you win?

Did the details or outcome of the argument still matter a day or two later? A month later?

Was it worth it?

How do you feel when you look back at those arguments now?

Reflect

Sometimes you have arguments with people about things that really matter. These could be about very important relationship or family issues; for example about different views on your children's education. They could be about principles and values that are important to you; for example your politics or religion. They could be about the ethos of your workplace or decisions about your working practices that have a significant effect on your quality of life; for example company goals or the patterns of shift work. They could even be about life and death; for example where people fight battles for or against abortion or voluntary euthanasia.

On the whole though, these really important debates are quite rare in everyday life.

Most of the time, the arguments that people have are about trivial things. They're about little things that really don't matter, like who did the washing up last ('I did it last night... no you didn't, I did it while you were watching TV... no you didn't, I wasn't watching TV last night... yes you were... no I wasn't... well, anyway I do it more often... no you don't... well, how many times did you do it last week?... four times at least... no you didn't!'). The arguments are about what colour to paint the hallway, or who left the top off the toothpaste tube. You get into fights about things getting broken, or forgotten or lost. Sometimes these are important but most often they're not really that important.

CASE STUDY

One day I came home from work to discover that my husband had broken a mug that was precious to me. It had been a gift. It was a very pretty, delicate china mug and it was one of my favourites. My husband apologized but still for a moment I really felt like having a good rant at him... how could he be so careless... I'd never be able to replace it... blah, blah, blah, etc. Then I stopped myself. The mug was gone, he felt bad and was sorry. Yes, I liked the mug and yes, it had some sentimental value. But it was, after all, just a mug. He on the other hand is a person, a person with feelings, the person I share my life with. And he, just like that mug and everything else, will not be here forever. I said, 'It's OK. It doesn't matter. Don't worry.'

How many times have you become involved in an argument that has settled into an ongoing feud that goes on and on? People have almost forgotten what they were upset about in the first place, but they're jolly well not going to go over to the other side to make up because, whatever it was about, they were... right!

These arguments that you have with people are all about control. You want them to do things the way you want them to because you're right. You want them to think the way you do because you're right. You want them to see that you're right and admit that you're right and agree with you, and you will keep on arguing until they do. In essence, you want to be in control of other people's minds and behaviour.

But ask yourself this. How many people do you actually *need* to agree with you and think you are right? To how many do you need to justify your views or behaviour? Of course there are some people whose agreement is important because their collaboration makes a big difference in your life. Who are these people? At home, perhaps your spouse or partner. Anyone else? At work, your line manager and perhaps a colleague who works closely with you. Anyone else? Probably not many others.

Also, ask yourself how many of the things that you argue about (even with those important few) really matter? Does it really matter who is right about who left the top off the toothpaste tube? Isn't the goal now to have a resolution for the future that suits everyone? Does it matter who did the washing up last night? Isn't making a plan for sharing the washing up in the future really the point now? And just how important is it for one person to win the battle of the colour of the hallway? Couldn't you just decide to keep searching for one that you both like?

As we discussed earlier, most people find it difficult to maintain confidence in themselves without some signs that other people like them. They also need other people to agree with them and go along with their views or suggestions in order to feel they have some control over their world and others. But, you really don't need everyone to agree with you.

Identify the people who really matter to you in your life. Engage in discussions with them and let go of your need to be in control of everyone else.

Earlier we said that people who need approval might become anxious in their car if another driver comes up very close behind them to indicate that they are going too slowly. We said they might even speed up a bit and drive faster than they would like so that someone won't be angry or think less of them.

On our courses, some people say 'I'd never do that; I'd put the brake on and drive even more slowly!'

For us, people who do this are simply replacing one stress-based action (approval-seeking) for another (battling for control). They think they gain control when they put on the brake. But who is really in control? We'd say the driver behind who managed to wind them up and got them to change the way they were driving in any way, whether to speed up or slow down.

So, if you let go of your need for approval (don't speed up) and your need for control (don't slow down), what action does that leave?

Choose the issues that truly concern you. Fight your corner on those issues and let go of your need to be in control of everything else.

If people (even the important ones) disagree, let them. If they want to do something differently from the way you would, let them. This is not about letting everything go and never having a say or fighting to have an influence. This is about letting some things go.

Let go when you recognize that the issue is not important to you and that you're just making an argument of it because you need to be in control and win. Let go even when the issue is important to you, but not as important as the other person's happiness or comfort. Let go when people pick arguments with you that you know are not worth having. Let go when people with no right or authority try to undermine your confidence by questioning or criticizing your strategies or decisions. If they have no authority, does it really matter if they think you're wrong? Before you get involved in a tiring discussion or argument ask yourself, 'If this person thinks I'm wrong how will that affect my life... really...?'

CASE STUDY

A while ago we ran a course that was open to participants from different organizations. The people who attended had never met each other before and would be unlikely to meet again. At this course we overheard two delegates, Brian and Wendy, talking during the lunch break. Brian was telling Wendy about some of the changes he had made at his organization. Wendy, who was from a different company said, 'Oh, well I wouldn't have done it like that. I don't think that will work.' Brian then spent his whole lunch break trying to persuade Wendy that he had done the right thing. He listed his reasons for the changes, and described the analysis and planning that had gone into the strategy in some detail. He was trying to persuade Wendy that he was right. Why? Did it really matter whether Wendy thought he was right or not? Did Wendy have any authority over Brian? No. Did she have any influence over Brian's future at work? No. Did she even have the knowledge and expertise to question Brian's strategies? Since she worked at a different organization, probably not. There would be some people that Brian would have to justify himself to. Wendy was not one of those people.

If Brian had been able to let go of his need to be in control and to win he could have relaxed and enjoyed his lunch. He could have saved his energy for the rest of the day and for the things he liked to do after work.

How could he have responded to Wendy instead of getting caught up in a time-consuming, energy-sapping argument?

We would suggest something like, 'That's interesting. I suppose time will tell if I have made the right decisions. Tell me more about the work that you do...'

Finally, remember that even when you engage in battles that you do think are worth the effort, you might still lose. Some things and some people's minds are not changeable no matter how hard you try, and there is nothing you can do about that. It's like bashing your head against a brick wall. Eventually all that happens is your head starts to hurt. If you are able to recognize when you're in a situation like that and can let go of your need for control and walk away, then you have the key to managing your stress levels at a very deep level.

Need for control – II

You need to be perfect

Wherever you look – television, magazines, movies, advertising boards – you will see images of perfection. The face with the perfect skin. The perfect house with the perfectly clean, tidy rooms and sparkling windows. The way that these images are captured in photographs make these perfections seem permanent. The skin never ages. The house never becomes messy or dirty even though a family with five children lives there. At one level everyone knows that these are illusions and it isn't really possible to be perfect. But at another level you seem to believe that perfection is possible, and that because it's possible, you must be a failure if you don't achieve it.

CASE STUDY

A friend who has a full-time job, a husband and three small children had a new patio laid at the front of her house. The patio was edged with beds of very attractive pebbles. It looked good. Pristine. Perfect in fact. Like something you would see in a 'Home and Garden' magazine. Our friend was delighted with the new layout. It was beautiful and we admired it with her too. Then one day we saw our friend outside vacuum cleaning her patio. Then we noticed that she seemed to vacuum or sweep or pick up leaves and other debris from her patio quite frequently. One day as we passed by her house we saw her standing in front of one of the pebble beds looking at it with a frown. There were tiny fallen leaves trapped in between the pebbles. We didn't stop to chat for long. It looked like it was going to be a busy morning for her. (Why did I tell you she has a husband and three small children?)

It is impossible to be in control of every aspect of your life. Trying to achieve the impossible is tiring and soul-destroying. If you need to be perfect you will become exhausted and stressed because you will always have a nagging sense of failure.

Can you be in control of some things? Yes. You just need to realize and accept that if you have control in your working life and achieve great success there, then something has to give at home. If you put home and family first then it isn't possible to put work first too. If you spend time playing with the children then you need to be able to accept that you won't have the time and energy also to keep the house and garden (and patio!) perfectly clean and tidy too. It isn't possible to maintain every aspect of life to the same level. Sometimes you just have to let something go.

If you feel bad about that because everywhere you look it appears that everyone else manages everything to perfection, just remind yourself that's an illusion. Everyone is struggling to balance conflicting demands and there will always be some areas that are a bit of a mess. The way to reduce your stress is to accept that. Spend time on the things that really matter to you and forgive yourself for the leaves on the patio.

CASE STUDY

Think about our stressed head teacher one last time. It turned out that she hadn't taken her holidays. We've said that part of the reason for that would be her need for approval. Having read the last section, could you complete the story?

The other part of the answer for this person was that she was trying to be in control to the point of keeping everything perfect. She needed to keep her eye on everything all the time and to do it all herself. She dared not go on holiday because then someone else would have to be in control for a while and they might not do it quite 'right', or they might let something 'slip through the net'. Of course 'right' meant 'the way she would do it', which meant 'perfectly'. She became stressed and completely burnt out because she needed everything to be perfect all of the time, and that's simply not possible.

This head teacher needed to let go of her needs for approval and control so that she could put into practice the stress-management strategy she already knew about – to take her holidays.

Need for control – III

YOU *need to know*

This third and final aspect of the need for control relates to people's need to be able to understand, explain and predict everything. It is easy to see how an ability to do that would lead to a sense of absolute control. If you can understand, explain and predict everything then you can prepare yourself and be able to cope with anything that comes along – you'll be ready for it all.

For instance, if you could predict for certain that the buyer of your house would pull out in a month's time then you would know what to do to prepare for that. If you knew for certain that the mortgage you needed would be agreed, then you wouldn't have to go through the stress of having to wait for another person to decide your future. As we've said before, if you could be in control of all aspects of moving house then this wouldn't be on your list of causes of stress.

The opposite of this ability to understand, explain and predict everything is to 'not know'. People are very uncomfortable with not knowing. You might recognize this as the well-known 'fear of the unknown' that people identify with so easily. People fear the unknown because it isn't possible to be in control of the unknown. How do you prepare? How do you avoid? How do you make sure things are as you want them to be?

How do you know you'll survive?

As we've said, at the level of instinct, people's need for control is about survival. As soon as you sense you are out of control your survival instinct (fight-or-flight) kicks in and your stress response is triggered, just as it would be if you had a sense of a tiger stalking you. Only, unlike a tiger, you can't fight a feeling of lack of control because there's nothing physical there to fight. So the only thing left is flight; to run away, to escape.

To escape a sense of lack of control people will make something up rather than accept that they don't know. The difficulty is that people who are vulnerable to stress will usually make something up that is negative or anxiety-provoking. They'll say to themselves, 'I bet our buyers will pull out', and then they'll feel stressed for the next six weeks waiting for that to happen. They're stressed because they have no control over this and can't stop it happening. Well it might happen. Then again, it might not. If it does they'll experience further pressure on top of a level of stress that has already built up and this will make the situation very much more difficult to deal with. If it doesn't they will have exhausted themselves with stress for no reason.

CASE STUDY

My husband, George, prides himself on being punctual. He hates to be late for anything. If he tells me he'll be home at 5.30 pm, he's home at 5.30 pm. If we arrange to meet out at a certain time, then he's there on the dot. This is good because I know that I can rely on him to be where he says he'll be when he says he'll be there. The down side comes if he's late.

One night he was very late home. There was no sign of him, no phone call and no message two hours after he said he would be home. I didn't know what had happened. My instinct to run away from the lack of control from not knowing took over and I made something up. I decided, knew for certain, that he'd had a terrible accident and was lying dead by the side of the road. In my mind I heard the news. I went to identify the body. I called my mother. I called his mother. I went to his funeral. In my mind I heard the speeches and the music at his funeral and I became distraught. I was shaking and crying. I thought about calling the police or ringing around hospitals but I was incapable.

Then... he arrived home. He had been stuck in a huge traffic jam and had been unable to contact me to let me know. I was in such a state by that time that it took me ages to calm down.

When I did, I thought to myself 'One day I might really lose him. When that day comes it will be terrible. I only want to go through that once.' I promised myself I would never do that again and I never have.

Now, if I don't know what has happened in any situation I say to myself, 'Don't kill George!' I don't know what has happened. When I do know, then I'll respond accordingly. Of course, I still get a bit worried or concerned when there are things that I didn't predict and can't explain. But that's not stress. It's just a normal, appropriate reaction.

Exercise six

How often have you told yourself things that have turned out not to be true? Take a few minutes to search out memories of times when you believed something about yourself, or other people, or your life as a whole, and then you found that what you believed wasn't true.

Think of everyday things like when you thought you wouldn't be able to find a parking space in town and you did; that the meal you cooked would flop and it was a great success; that you wouldn't be able to complete a task or project and you did; that your friend didn't want to know you any more because they hadn't called you, but then it turned out that they had just been very busy.

Also, think about those aspects of life that have had a greater impact, like when you thought that you would never find a new relationship and then you did; that no one would ever employ you and they did; that you wouldn't be able to cope with a difficult time, and you did.

> It is easy to think of times when what you told yourself was true; for example, when you said there'd be no parking spaces and you were right. This is easy because you naturally focus on the experiences that reinforce your beliefs in order to regain your sense of control. But, the reality is that for every time you were right you will have been wrong. If you focus more on the times that you were wrong you might find it easier to say 'I don't know'.

Reflect

A lot of the time people's stress levels rise because they are responding emotionally to things they imagine rather than to what is actually happening.

Managing stress is often about accepting that you can't read minds, predict the future or know what is happening when you're not there.

It can be a great relief to let go of your need to be in control and to be able to say, 'I don't know. When I know, I'll deal with it.' Whenever you find yourself worrying about, or becoming upset about what might be happening or what might happen in the future, remind yourself, DON'T KILL GEORGE!

We hope you can see how your need for control is a powerful factor underlying your stress.

It is your need for control that makes living with children stressful. You want to be in control of their mental and physical well-being, and quite often that's just not possible as they begin to go out into an unpredictable world.

It is your need for control that makes managing family relationships so stressful. People have minds of their own. They'll have their own disputes, break-ups and make-ups, and often you will have very little influence over all of that.

Your need for control underlies any stress you feel over the environment in which you live. You can often have very little control over what happens in your immediate environment and this extends to global environmental concerns. For example, you might have very strong feelings about environmental and other global issues and this passion will motivate you to do what you can to make whatever impact you can on your area of interest. Do all that you can with commitment and drive. Remember though, passion is different from stress. When does passion become stress? When you need to be in control. If you need to be in control of the bigger picture this can easily lead to feelings of powerlessness and despair and you may give up altogether.

What about bereavement? How does stress arise in this situation? Grief becomes stress when people find it difficult to accept that the loss of the people they love is something that they can have no control over. Grief becomes stress when they have to know why, or when they imagine that there was something they could have done to change the course of events so that person would still be alive. The death of a loved one is the ultimate challenge to your need for control and it's hard to live with something that is so completely out of your hands.

Look back to the list of causes of stress that you wrote earlier and see if you can identify others that have any of the three aspects of the need for control at the heart of them. If you can let go of that need for control, even just occasionally, this will help you to deal with stress at a much deeper level than any aromatherapy massage will reach.

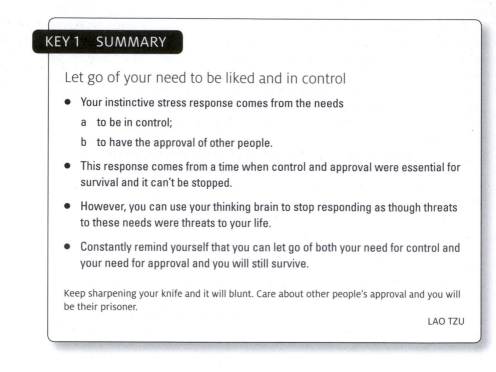

KEY 1   SUMMARY

Let go of your need to be liked and in control

- Your instinctive stress response comes from the needs
  a to be in control;
  b to have the approval of other people.

- This response comes from a time when control and approval were essential for survival and it can't be stopped.

- However, you can use your thinking brain to stop responding as though threats to these needs were threats to your life.

- Constantly remind yourself that you can let go of both your need for control and your need for approval and you will still survive.

Keep sharpening your knife and it will blunt. Care about other people's approval and you will be their prisoner.

LAO TZU

KEY 2

07

Live your values

Often people say they value certain things and then put their energy into something else. Spend your time and energy on the most important things in your life, and avoid the urgent distractions.

A model to develop awareness

Urgent and important

Each activity you engage in during the course of a day, from brushing your teeth to dealing with a complicated client or family issue, can be described in two ways:

1 how urgent the activity is;

and

2 how important the activity is.

If the activity is 'urgent', this means you are doing something that demands *immediate attention*. An example of this might be answering a telephone. When a phone rings you don't say 'I think I'll answer that phone tomorrow.' It will ring a limited number of times and then stop, and you will have missed that call if you don't pick it up right away. So, a ringing telephone has a sense of urgency that requires action. Another example might be if you hear a fire or smoke alarm. You wouldn't sit back and decide to react later. You would act straight away to investigate the cause or escape danger.

Something is urgent if it can't wait until later, or tomorrow or next week. It has to be done right now.

On the other hand, if the activity is 'important', this means that what you are doing *delivers something for you in terms of your personal values and goals*. It is an activity that takes you closer to fulfilling your dreams and ambitions, or enables you to look after the people, relationships and possessions that are most precious to you. So, these activities might range from learning a new language to rushing a loved-one to hospital after an accident. Whatever your own personal aims are in life, if you do something towards achieving those then you are doing something important.

That distinction seems simple and straightforward. But if you look closely you'll see that the picture becomes more complicated. The two concepts, 'urgent' and 'important', are linked in quite an intricate way.

Building the picture

Take a look at the two very different activities we mentioned above when we described what we meant by 'urgent'; answering the telephone and reacting to a fire or smoke alarm. Even though they both fit into the urgent category of activities, would you say they have the same quality of urgency?

Let's put it this way. If a telephone started ringing and a fire alarm went off at the same time, which would you respond to and which would you ignore?

You would react first to the one that delivers the outcome you judge to be more 'important' (ie delivers something for you in terms of your personal values and goals).

Now, it isn't for us to say what would or wouldn't, or should or shouldn't, be most important to you. But let's assume you value your life more highly than the need to answer the phone, in which case we guess you would react first to the fire alarm.

Both the fire alarm and the ringing phone are urgent, but when you react to the fire alarm and ignore the phone, in that moment your judgement is that it is more important to protect your life than it is to find out who is calling you.

> We might say that reacting to a fire alarm is URGENT AND IMPORTANT while answering the phone is URGENT AND NOT IMPORTANT.

NB. This doesn't mean that a telephone call is never important. A phone call certainly could be important if the caller had something crucial to tell you. It just means, in that particular moment, compared to saving your life, it is not important – whatever the caller had to say to you.

In the same way, look at the different examples we gave when we described what we meant by 'important': learning a new language and rushing a loved-one to hospital after an accident. Both of these are activities that might be important to someone, but do they both have the same quality of importance?

Imagine that while you are studying your language textbook you hear a loud crash. You rush out to find that your partner has fallen off a ladder and is crying out in pain. What would you do? You would react to the one that you judge to be more urgent (ie it can't wait until later, or tomorrow or next week. It has to be done right now).

Again, it's not for us to say what your judgements would or should be in any situation, but we could probably assume that you wouldn't go back and finish your studies before seeing to your injured partner. We guess that you would simply rush to your partner and take immediate action to comfort them and get them to the hospital as quickly as possible.

Learning a new language and the well-being of your partner might both be important to you, but in this situation your judgement is that your partner's well-being is more urgent than the need to complete your studies for the day.

In this case we could say that taking your partner to hospital is

IMPORTANT AND URGENT (the same as URGENT AND IMPORTANT above).

While learning a new language is

IMPORTANT AND NOT URGENT.

From our two main categories of 'urgent' and 'important', we have now developed three categories with examples of each as follows:

URGENT AND IMPORTANT – reacting to a fire alarm; rushing a loved-one to hospital.

URGENT AND NOT IMPORTANT – answering the telephone.

IMPORTANT AND NOT URGENT – learning a new language.

We just need to add one more category to complete the picture. We're sure you can work out what that is. Perhaps you could write it down here before we tell you:

....

The last category is for those things that you do during the course of a day that have neither to be done immediately (no one will be hurt and there will be no dire consequences if you delay) nor do they get you any closer to realizing your values or to achieving your life's aims and ambitions. They're the things that you do to waste time instead of doing important things that are often more difficult or challenging. They're things that you drift into doing without any real goal or even desire. They're the hanging around, the aimless pottering about and the zoning out. These kinds of things might include hours spent watching soaps or reality TV. They especially include watching the programmes you flick through after the ones that you specifically tuned in for because you can't be bothered to switch off the TV and get on with something else (this is not a criticism – we all do it!). They're the time spent on computer games, Facebook and Twitter. They're the often enjoyable, relaxing and distracting things that might fit into the category of

NOT IMPORTANT AND NOT URGENT.

CASE STUDY

This evening I've been able to find all kinds of things to do instead of settling down to write this chapter. I've 'treated myself' to an extra episode of a TV series I'm enjoying on DVD at the moment, tidied my e-mail folders, replied to a couple of texts, made a phone call, answered a phone call, deleted voicemail messages, reorganized my CDs in a 'better' order, made a cup of tea, wiped down the kitchen surfaces... again. One of the activities mentioned in this box is most important to me and it's the one I kept putting off. But I got a lot done didn't I? Is this kind of behaviour ringing any bells with you?

We now have four categories of activity: Urgent and Important, Urgent and Not Important, Important and Not Urgent, and Not Important and Not Urgent. You will be able to fit everything you do, every day and night, into one of these categories. That's exactly what we're going to ask you to do.

Exercise seven

'The matrix'

Below we have mapped the four categories of activity onto a matrix diagram. This concept was first introduced by the writer Stephen Covey in his famous book *The 7 Habits of Highly Effective People* (these habits are not the same as our 7 KEYS).

As you can see, it is now possible to think of your daily activities as existing in one of four quadrants:

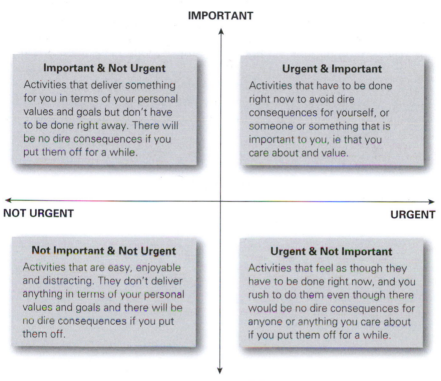

IMPORTANT

Important & Not Urgent

Activities that deliver something for you in terms of your personal values and goals but don't have to be done right away. There will be no dire consequences if you put them off for a while.

Urgent & Important

Activities that have to be done right now to avoid dire consequences for yourself, or someone or something that is important to you, ie that you care about and value.

NOT URGENT ← → **URGENT**

Not Important & Not Urgent

Activities that are easy, enjoyable and distracting. They don't deliver anything in terms of your personal values and goals and there will be no dire consequences if you put them off.

Urgent & Not Important

Activities that feel as though they have to be done right now, and you rush to do them even though there would be no dire consequences for anyone or anything you care about if you put them off for a while.

NOT IMPORTANT

Your next task will be to fill in a blank matrix with the activities that occupy you. To achieve that, over the next few days and nights, make a list of everything you do (including sleeping, eating, washing, housework, workplace and social activities, etc). You might write the activity down as you are doing it, about to do it, immediately after, or you might take stock every hour or so. Once you have a completed list, for each activity ask yourself:

1 Is this something I had to do (or felt I had to do) right away without any delay at all? If the answer is 'yes', then write 'urgent' beside the item. If the answer is 'no', then write 'not urgent' beside it.

2 Is this something that took me closer to fulfilling my personal values and achieving my life's goals and ambitions? If the answer is 'yes', then write 'important' beside the item. If 'no', then write 'not important'.

For example, let's suppose you spent most of a morning ploughing your way through a backlog of 50 e-mails. Maybe there was a sense of urgency about this. After all, you couldn't let them pile up forever and it would be discourteous to delay the delivery of a response to people. So your answer to question 1 might be 'yes' and therefore 'urgent'. On the other hand, how effectively will responding to these e-mails take you closer to your personal goals for your life, career, relationships? The chances are that most of the time you spent doing this did not deliver much along these lines. If that is the case the answer to question 2 will be 'no', and therefore 'not important'.

(NB we are not suggesting that these will or should be the way you evaluate spending time on e-mails – it's just an example. You need to be completely honest with your lists and the way that you place your activities in each of the quadrants.)

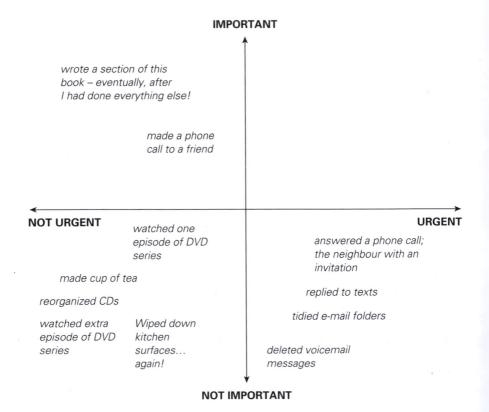

When you have answered these questions for each activity on your list you should be able quite easily to transfer each item onto the appropriate quadrant of the matrix. It is fine just to write the item down anywhere in the quadrant. However, if you want to be more detailed you can show not only that something is urgent or important, but also how urgent or important it is. The more urgent something feels, the further towards the right of the matrix it will appear. The more important it is, the higher on the matrix you should place it. Opposite is an example to demonstrate, using the activities of one of my evenings that I described in the case study. While you might judge the place of these activities differently, it is only my evaluation that counts for me. When you complete yours it will be only your evaluation that counts for you.

Here is your blank matrix to fill in. If it starts to get crowded you might like to sketch this diagram onto further sheets of paper so that you could use one for each day.

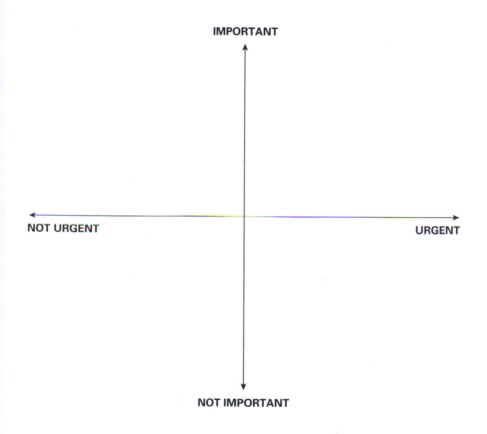

IMPORTANT

NOT URGENT

URGENT

NOT IMPORTANT

Reflect

Let's take a look at what you've written in your four quadrants.

Urgent and Important

What have you entered as Urgent and Important? If you had to evacuate your home or workplace building because there was a fire, then that would certainly be here. Was it important to save your life? Absolutely. Was it something that had to be done without delay? Of course. Other things that have a legitimate place in this quadrant might be responding to a client or family crisis. Other possible entries might relate to tight deadlines for important work projects or the rushed payment of final bills to ensure continued delivery of essential utilities.

Any activity in this quadrant will have an element of stress attached to it. That's because, if you are doing something that falls into this category, there will be a strong sense that either you or someone you care about is in imminent danger. This is the true stress response that is appropriate when you are dealing with potential threats to survival. Because of the element of stress involved here, ideally you will visit this quadrant very rarely.

Of course, for some people it is not possible to keep out of the Urgent and Important quadrant; for example, those whose job involves protecting others or reacting to emergencies and life-or-death situations. It is well known that people in these kinds of professions experience high levels of stress. You will also find it difficult to keep out of this area if you have an illness or injury that worsens or flares up frequently, or is life-threatening, or if you are taking care of someone else who does. Therefore you will also very likely have to handle raised levels of stress. If you are in either of these groups then please pay careful attention to the 7 KEYS – you definitely need to put them into action to build your resilience.

Fortunately, for most people real life-threatening crises and emergencies occur very infrequently and so it is possible for them to keep out of the Urgent and Important quadrant for most of the time. If you are not one of the exceptions mentioned in the box above you should have very few, if any, entries in this quadrant. Yet, when we do this exercise at our face-to-face courses people tend to put a lot of activities here. If you have entered many activities in this space then take a careful look to double-check.

Often people behave as though much of what they do is both urgent and important, and they experience chronic stress as a result. But careful examination shows that many of these things are not really urgent, and/or they're not really important. Put simply, no one is going to suffer or die if this thing is not done right now.

When people look carefully at the items they've put in this quadrant they can see that the activities are in fact important, but they are only urgent because they weren't dealt with earlier. For example, family or client crises often (not always, but often) only become crises because potential conflict or need for support and attention weren't met earlier. It's the same with, for example, rushed payment of bills or tight work deadlines. Often (again not always, but often) they've only become emergencies because you left them till the last minute. Things that start in the Important and Not Urgent quadrant migrate to the Urgent and Important quadrant if they are continually postponed. Like this...

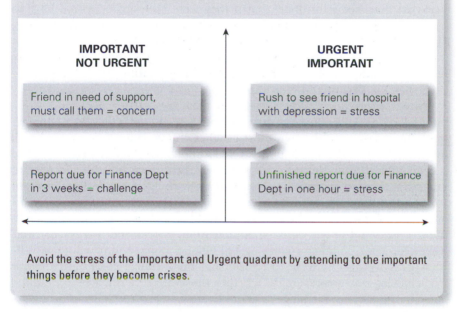

IMPORTANT NOT URGENT

Friend in need of support, must call them = concern

Report due for Finance Dept in 3 weeks = challenge

URGENT IMPORTANT

Rush to see friend in hospital with depression = stress

Unfinished report due for Finance Dept in one hour = stress

Avoid the stress of the Important and Urgent quadrant by attending to the important things before they become crises.

So when people stop to analyse what they are doing it turns out that they are becoming stressed about things that are not worth becoming stressed about. Look again at your Urgent and Important quadrant. Do you become stressed by things that are not worth becoming stressed about?

Are you becoming stressed about things that should be in another quadrant?

Urgent and Not Important

How about the Urgent and Not Important quadrant? If you are being strictly honest you are likely to find that a lot of what you do fits in here. We would say that most of people's time is consumed by meetings, e-mails, texts, phone calls, journeys, errands, etc. These are things that have a sense of urgency. The phone rings, you feel the need to pick up right away. A text or e-mail comes through, you feel the need to check it and respond immediately. You are called into a meeting about something or asked to run an errand that you know will take up time without achieving much, but still you go immediately. You've planned to spend time on a project or activity that is important to you but you drop it when someone asks you to do something else that is important to them.

All of these are examples of things that are urgent because there is a sense that they must be done right away. However, as we've discovered, these activities are very rarely important – unless you are one of the exceptions whose job involves protecting others or reacting to emergencies as we described above.

For most people it is very easy to fill the day with urgent activities and to feel that they 'got a lot done', but if they were honest they would have to admit that these activities did not save or protect their lives or anyone else's. They did not protect or save anything of great value to them. They did not take them closer to achieving their greater life's goals and ambitions. So, instead of finding a place in the Urgent and Important quadrant, they need to be here, in Urgent and Not Important.

Now, people don't like to feel that they are wasting time or rushing around to no good purpose so they prefer to describe what they do as 'important'. But it's ok to admit that most of what you do is not important. You'll notice in my own example I put 'answered a phone call', 'replied to texts', 'tidied e-mail folders' and 'deleted voicemails' in the Urgent and Not Important quadrant. I could try to tell myself that these things were really important so I had to do them instead of writing this book. That would reassure me that I wasn't just wasting time, but it would be untrue. Like me, your life is mostly made up of the daily communication, chores and workplace tasks that keep your home and working life ticking along, and it will always be that way. We all just have to realize that these things don't get us closer to achieving our greater goals, whether those are to write a book, build a relationship, learn a language or climb Everest. In fact they give us an excuse to delay those important things, and, if we let this quadrant get too full, we'll never get the chance to do them.

Not Important and Not Urgent

Then there's the Not Important and Not Urgent quadrant. We'd say there would probably be a lot in here, too. Activities in this quadrant are the recreational things; watching TV, chatting, chilling out. There is no pressure to do these things, and they generally don't move you closer to achieving the important aims of your life. They are pleasant activities that are enjoyable only for their own sake. It would be a shame if there were no such activities in your life. Everybody needs downtime and to have fun sometimes.

You might even say that a certain amount of this should be in one of the Important quadrants. You won't be able to tackle the more valued and difficult areas of your life if you are burnt out because you never take time to relax your mind and body. So you might say that it is important to do these things because it is good for your health. You might even say that it is important and urgent if your health has already suffered from high stress without a break and you are at a point where you must take some time out without delay. In those cases the activities should be in the appropriate Important quadrant.

The entries in Not Important and Not Urgent are those things you do even though you don't need to; for example, watching an extra episode of a programme simply because you can't be bothered to get up after the first one, sorting out CDs and mindlessly wiping already-clean kitchen surfaces as I did. It's fine to do these things, too, up to a point. But, again, if you let this quadrant become too full, it will be at the expense of your more highly valued aims, which will never be achieved. After all, if I hadn't eventually stopped pottering about, this chapter would never have been finished – and wouldn't that have been a shame?!

Important and Not Urgent

Finally, let's look at the Important and Not Urgent quadrant. Remember from our earlier description, these are activities that deliver something for you in terms of your personal values and goals. They take you closer to fulfilling your dreams and ambitions, or enable you to look after the people, relationships and possessions that are most precious to you. However, although these things are important, they are not urgent, therefore they can be postponed. Things in this quadrant are very often enjoyable and satisfying. However, they also tend to be physically and/or emotionally more challenging, so it can be very tempting to do just that – to put them off. For example, if you have children or a partner it is probably important to you to spend some quality time with them. Is it urgent? No, it can be postponed until you have got all of those e-mails out of the way. Long-term ambitions might include, for example, learning to play the piano. Is it important? Absolutely, it would be powerfully life-enhancing. Is it urgent? Certainly not, it will just have to wait until you've finished doing the dishes and making some phone calls.

How well-populated is this section of your matrix? Congratulations if you have some entries here and have spent a reasonable amount of time on them (we won't know, so you must be honest with yourself). It means that you are clear what your values are in life, and are able to prioritize your activities so you can make time for those. If you find that you haven't been able to do much that would fit in here then you need to ask yourself 'why?' Take a few moments to think about it and we will come back to this question shortly.

Balancing the quadrants

The most meaningful and valuable things you could be doing with your time are in the top Important quadrants, the Important and Not Urgent, and Urgent and Important.

When a crisis occurs that threatens you or the people and things you cherish most, you drop everything you are doing that would fit in any of the other quadrants and take action that is Urgent and Important. You have to do this, and you would.

Once you have seen to any emergencies, it would make sense to keep prioritizing things that are important to you; things that bring you closer to achieving your goals and realizing your dreams and ambitions. However, it seems that's not what people generally do. Instead of being drawn towards importance, they are lured by urgency. They postpone those important things because they can, and instead they spend their time doing things that are Urgent and Not Important.

Then, they allow themselves to indulge in the Not Important and Not Urgent recreational aspects of their lives.

Finally, they turn their attention to the activities that will deliver most to them personally, yet can be delayed, ie those that are Important and Not Urgent.

So, we could say that people tend to manage the activities and tasks in their lives in this order:

Urgent and Important

Urgent and Not Important

Not Important and Not Urgent

Important and Not Urgent

In other words, people attend to what they value most... last! That means they tackle the things that are most meaningful and will get them closer to their much-desired goals when they have least time and are most tired. That is certainly what happened to me when I postponed writing in order to do less important things. As it got later and later I became more and more exhausted, and I was able to spend less time writing than I had planned.

Now, we would not suggest that you do nothing at all in the Not Important quadrants. As we've said, things in the Important and Not Urgent quadrant, while enjoyable and satisfying, are often mentally, physically and/or emotionally quite challenging. So it would be possible to become worn out if you did nothing that was less demanding from time to time. I need to relax in front of the TV or potter in the kitchen sometimes so I can come back to writing with refreshed energy.

CASE STUDY

A friend has just achieved a very important goal of his. It was to walk the 214 Wainwright Fells in the Lake District. His aim was to finish them in two years (it usually takes a lot longer). Although he could have put off some of his walks to do something that was less strenuous from time to time, he was so committed to his self-imposed deadline that he had to spend nearly all his free time in his Important and Not Urgent quadrant, with very little time to rest and relax during that two-year period. As a result he put his mind and body under immense strain and was completely exhausted by the end. He became unfocused and withdrawn. His immune system was undermined so he became ill frequently and had wounds from walking that became infected and wouldn't heal. It took him months to recover. Now he is the first to say 'That's not the way to do it.'

In any case, it would be a sad life that was stripped of all frivolous pleasure, and sometimes you will wish to be responsive to the everyday personal and workplace demands that come your way, even if they don't deliver much to you personally.

What we would suggest is that you consider re-balancing the way you allocate your attention between the quadrants so that the entries each day reflect more closely your own set of values and priorities. Balance is the crucial element. Do things in the Not Important quadrants, but take care to keep some (most if possible) of your time and energy for the things that matter most to you. It is absolutely vital to do this if you want to maintain your resilience. We will tell you why in the next chapter.

CASE STUDY

Recently we met a delegate who had been on a previous course in which we had presented KEY 2 and the Important and Urgent Matrix. He told us this had been a moment of revelation for him. He realized he had had a very clear goal in life for a long time: it was important to him to get fit. However, he'd kept postponing it because it was not urgent. It was always in the 'maybe next week' category. Then he scrutinized the entries on his matrix and noticed that there were a lot of things in the Not Important and Not Urgent quadrant. He could see that this was because his way of relaxing was to watch every TV soap opera. He decided that if he gave up just one of the soaps he could free up enough time to go to the gym three times a week. That's what he did. When we met again he was healthy, fighting fit, and rightly pleased with himself.

Back to the question

Earlier we asked you to think about a question. We said if you hadn't been able to do much that would fit into the Important and Not Urgent quadrant then you need to ask yourself 'why?' There are a number of possible answers to this question.

1. Lack of goal clarity

Perhaps you do not have a set of clear goals for your life that you can use to guide the way you prioritize what you do. If that's the case for you, then we would strongly recommend that you take some time out to think carefully about what is meaningful and worthwhile to you and draw up a set of such goals. Think about who you are and who you want to be. What and who is most precious to you? How do you want to demonstrate these ideals in your daily life?

If you don't have a way of living according to your own values you could find that you are living only according to other people's values. Simply, you could find that other people are running your life. This is a profound source of chronic stress. We'll explain why in the next chapter. For now, because this is such a powerful source of stress, we would like you to do something about it before you read the next chapter. In fact we'd like you to do this even before you go on with this one.

Exercise eight

It might be useful to do this exercise even if you do have a degree of clarity about your goals. You can use it as a reminder to refresh your commitment and motivation.

We'd like you to take a few moments or hours, even days, however long it takes, to get some sense of what you might wish to do that you would find fulfilling and stimulating, and that would enable you to develop a sense of accomplishment and self-worth.

They could be grand, life-transforming dreams and ambitions that will take a long time to achieve; but they don't have to be. They might just be small things that may appear insignificant to others but that would be meaningful and life-enhancing to you.

Also, look at all of the different areas of your life: family, career, finance, spirituality, health, friends, hobbies, society, community, etc. Which aspects are most important to you, and how would you like to reflect that importance in the way you allocate your time and energy? You don't have to have it all mapped out in fine detail. Just make a start with some general ideas that give you a feeling of determination and motivation.

NB It is crucial that you write down things that really are of value to you, not things that you think should be of value. The latter is a judgement based on what you believe other people might think and the purpose of this exercise is to move you away from living according to other people's values. So don't ask yourself, 'Is this a "good" value or ambition?' Just ask 'Is this a value that I truly hold and would like to reflect in the way I behave?', or, 'Is this an ambition that I would really like to achieve, for my own pleasure, pride or satisfaction?'

Make a note of your thoughts here:

....

....

....

Now read on.

2. Other obstacles

We don't wish to be disheartening at this stage; however, it is important to recognize that even when you have clarity about your goals it can still be difficult to achieve them, or even to make a start towards achieving them. You know what you would like to spend time on but somehow you never quite manage to get into that Important and Not Urgent space. Once you are aware of the potential obstacles then you will be able to overcome them.

Let's consider those things that typically obstruct people's path to achieving their personal goals:

i. You don't have the time

People lead busy lives. They rush through their activities, always aware of the other tasks that are queuing up to be done.

You may have observed from Exercise Seven that most of your frenetic urgency actually achieves very little in terms of reflecting your own values and achieving your core aims. Like many areas of life, you might recognize the 80/20 rule operating here; this is the idea that 80 per cent of what people achieve is the result of 20 per cent of their effort. The remainder delivers very little, it is just habitual busyness.

We hope you are clearer now about what you really want to achieve in your life, at least for the time being. Now you have to do it; not by squeezing more and more into an already impossible schedule, but by being cleverer with the time you have.

You can't spend less time doing things that are genuinely Urgent and Important because these things just have to be done right away. So, like our delegate who gave up one of his TV soaps to go to the gym, you need to be smarter with the time you spend in the bottom half of the matrix (remember, these quadrants contain things that you do even though they don't deliver results, they just keep you feeling occupied).

We face this challenge ourselves when we take on a new and sizeable task. For example, writing this book. To clear the considerable time this requires, we have to examine the way we work. Is it really necessary to respond to every e-mail the moment it comes through? No. So we go offline for a while. That way we are not distracted by the sound of e-mails coming in and drawn by the sense of urgency we would feel to read and reply to the e-mail immediately. Could some of those phone calls go to voicemail to be attended to in the afternoon? Yes. So we switch the phone to silent. Again, this helps us avoid the ring that would lead us to pick up right away. Since our offices are based in our homes we are subject to other distractions too, as I was in my earlier example. Did I really need to wipe the kitchen surfaces, watch another episode of the DVD and sort out my CDs before I got down to the task of writing? No. What I really needed was to write first, then indulge in the other things if I still had the energy.

CASE STUDY

Perhaps you are asking yourself, 'What if one of the phone calls or e-mails we miss turns out to have been Urgent and Important once we get to them?' It's a good question. It is possible of course. But isn't there always a chance at any time, for anybody, that this could happen?

One afternoon, some years ago, my brother called to tell me that my father had been rushed to hospital. I couldn't answer the phone at the moment he called because I was teaching. I picked up the message too late to be there when my father died.

This kind of experience is tragic. But you can't live your life waiting by the phone or staring at your e-mail inbox in case a crisis arises.

People feel they must have their eye on the ball at all times and keep 'on top of things' every second. That's because they need to be 'in control'. KEY 1 explained this need and the reality that it simply isn't possible to be in control of everything all the time. Sometimes you have to let go and focus on the important task at hand. You have to get on with your life. If you miss something that turns out to be more important and urgent, that will be dreadful, maybe even tragic. And you'll deal with it. At some time or another, like me, you probably already have.

Obviously, each individual will have to examine their personal scope for finding time. Somewhere in the bottom half of that matrix there will be some time to spare. If there isn't, then your life is already in perfect balance!

ii. Your dreams and ambitions are too big to achieve

Sometimes people's life-goals involve a substantial amount of preparation or work and would take a long time to complete. If you revisit your list of goals, you might well find that you are being held back by the sense that they might be just too daunting to tackle. You have established what you would like to achieve and why, but now the *how* is getting in the way.

Of course, it is perfectly legitimate to hold your goals up to a reality test. It might genuinely be the case that you want to do things you simply cannot accomplish. I'd love to be able to climb to the top of Everest, but I know I'll never be able to. It would be unrealistic to set that as one of my goals, and that's fine. More often than not though, people are limited by a mental barrier. If this is the case for you, remember what the Chinese philosopher Confucius said, 'A journey of a thousand miles begins with a single step.'

Break big tasks down into bite-size chunks. The excuse that you don't have time to learn to play the piano or to speak a new language would be valid if you expected full mastery by tomorrow. The reality is that you always can embark on that first step. You can clear enough time to enrol on the course, book a lesson, learn a few words, practise for half an hour. Grand ambitions are achieved by taking one step, then another, then another. While you are enjoying the journey, gradually, step by small step, you'll get there. But, you have to start.

iii. Other people

Sadly, other people will often try to interfere with your ambitions and aspirations. They may be parents who can't accept that their child is moving far from the nest. They may be friends who don't want to lose you from their safe, comfortable circle. They may be colleagues who are jealous of the possibility that you will be freer or more successful than they are. They may be partners who fear you won't have enough time left for them and they will be neglected. Whatever their motivation, if you come up with an audacious, innovative, exciting plan for your future growth, the chances are there will be someone whose aim is to try to talk you out of it.

There are a number of ways you might tackle this. One is to avoid those who seek to discourage you. However, you may not be able to do this. Family, friends and colleagues are generally an inescapable part of life. Although their negativity might be a problem, nevertheless they could be people you need and perhaps love, and you don't want to turn away from them.

Another approach could be to try to change those people's attitudes and get them to be more supportive. Well, that's possible. But sometimes people have a very strong investment in keeping you as you are so they will stick to their position in spite of your explanations and persuasion.

That leaves only one remaining option. If you can't change other people, you have to change yourself. If you are allowing others to hold you back from the direction you really desire for your life, then you will have to find a way to stand up to their negative influence and do it anyway.

This is much easier to say than to do. In fact, it may be one of the most challenging things you will have to practise as you work towards managing your stress levels more effectively.

In the next chapter we will show you the skills and qualities you need to resist the negativity of others and achieve KEY 2. But we are aware that, even when you know what these skills and qualities are, you might still not put them into practice – because it can be very hard to do!

Why do you think it might be so difficult to stand up to the influence of other people, even once we've shown you how to do it? (Think back to KEY 1 for the answer to this question.)

It's difficult because people instinctively need the approval of others. When you decide to act against the wishes or views of other people you risk losing their approval. That is extremely hard to do because it goes against your instinct. It takes you far out of your comfort zone and therefore, at least to begin with, you might feel quite anxious or uncertain, perhaps even fearful. So, as well as having the skills to stand up to others you will also need to be powerfully motivated to live outside of your comfort zone for a while so that you can put those skills into practice. As well as the skills you need, we will do our best to give you that motivation too.

Before you go on to the next chapter and find out how we will do that, see if you can work out for yourself what that motivation might be.

What would it take to get you to step out of your comfort zone and endure the discomfort you may experience when you begin to stand up to the negative influence of others? Why do you absolutely have to start, right now, to live your life according to your own values in the way that you want to, and that you believe will lead to your greatest chance of happiness and fulfilment even though others might try to stop you?

At our face-to-face courses we usually take our lunch break here so people have some time to think this over and come back with their answer. Perhaps you could do the same. Take a break, think about it, and write down your answer here:

....

....

....

Live your values

- All activities can be described in two ways:
  1 how urgent they are;
  2 how important they are.

- Urgent activities demand instant attention. Important activities deliver something of value to you.

- People often spend a lot of their time doing things that are urgent but not important. They feel busy but don't get closer to their life-goals.

- The key is to achieve a balance in life, so that the busyness of everyday life doesn't distract you from progressing towards your personal values and goals.

How different our lives are when we really know what is deeply important to us, and keeping that picture in mind, we manage ourselves each day to be and to do what really matters most.

STEPHEN COVEY

KEY 3

08

> ## You have a right to determine your own life
>
> *You have the right to control everything you do, feel and think. Once you accept that, then you have real power in your life. Develop empathetic assertiveness and stand up for your own rights.*

At the end of the last chapter we said we would guide you towards the skills and qualities you need to put KEY 2 into practice. Here you can see that these are embedded in our KEY 3. They are the skills and qualities of EMPATHETIC ASSERTIVENESS. In this chapter we will explore this concept in some depth.

However, we also said we are aware that, even when you know what these skills and qualities are, you might still not put them into practice. That's because to do so means you might act in a way that is against the views and wishes of other people, and that can be very difficult to do. It may take you out of your comfort zone and so cause you to feel anxiety and maybe even fear. So you're going to need some very strong motivation to help you over the comfort-zone barrier. We aim to impart that motivation even before we look at the skills you need to develop. By the time we get there, you'll be ready to overcome any anxieties or fears you might experience and keen to get started.

We challenged you to see if you could work out what that motivation might be, and asked the question:

> *Why do you absolutely have to start right now to live your life according to your own values, in the way that you want to, and that you believe will lead to your greatest chance of happiness and fulfilment?*

Our answer to the question is simply... because life is short!

Life is short – getting motivated

For KEY 2 we invited you to use a matrix diagram to look at the way you spend your time. The matrix will have shown you to what extent you are focusing your energy on the things that are most important to you. We'd like to explore that a bit more deeply now.

Exercise nine

We're going to ask a very simple straightforward question now. We'd like you to write your answer in big letters in the box below the question. The answer to the question is either 'YES' or 'NO'. We don't want any explanations or reasons. Just 'YES' or 'NO'.

The question is

Are you spending most of your time and energy on the things that are most important to you?

Now write down one word, sentence or phrase to reflect how you feel now having answered that question (again, don't give any explanations or reasons for your answer, just say how you *feel*).

....

....

....

Reflect

Obviously we don't know how you responded to our question, or how you feel about your answer. But here are some points for you to consider:

1. Most often people do not spend most of their time and energy on the things that they value most.

At our live courses we find most people discover that they are not spending most of their time and energy on the things they say are most important to them. So if you are in that position (you have written 'NO' in the box above) you need to be aware that you are certainly not on your own.

2. Most people who write 'NO' in their box say they feel sad or guilty about that.

When we ask people how they feel at the end of the exercise, we find that the few who can write 'YES' in their box feel quite comfortable and content with themselves. Occasionally people who write 'NO' say that they feel ok too, but this is very rare. They most often say they feel sad and/or guilty. They feel sad because they have a sense of loss, and guilty because they begin to judge themselves as 'wrong' and 'bad'. They have a sense that it must be 'wrong' to neglect the most important thing in their life while they do something else, and that therefore they must be 'bad' for doing so.

Our KEY 1 showed that people need to be 'good' (to gain approval) and 'right' (to be in control). So these feelings of being 'bad' and 'wrong' lead people to become defensive and to try to convince everyone, including themselves, that they are really 'good' and 'right'. This usually takes the form of, 'Well, I have to do all those other things in order to take care of the most important thing' or 'But that's how it has to be in the real world' and so on.

If this is you, we would encourage you to stop trying to justify yourself. The way you are running your life is not 'wrong', nor is it 'bad'. It simply is as it is, and there will be very good reasons for the way that you are managing your life now. In many cases it just isn't possible for people to spend all, or even most of their time and energy on the things they value most. For example, your family might be the most valuable thing in your life but you still have to spend a lot of your time at work if you need to earn a living to take care of them. On the other hand, your work and professional or financial ambitions might be the most important things to you, but you still have to spend some time with your family and friends if you want to maintain your relationships with them too.

But here is another question. This is most relevant to you if you answered 'NO' in the box, but take a look at it even if you wrote 'YES'. You might find it useful to think about sometime in the future if you find yourself in a different position.

This is a hypothetical question about a scenario that we hope will never actually happen to you. Here it is:

If you were told today that you have only six months to live, how long would it take for you to start to re-balance the way you allocate your time and energy so that you could answer 'YES'?

In our groups the answer to that question is always... always... 'No time at all'. Is that your response too?

Now think about this: how do you know you haven't got only another six months to live? How do you know you've *even* got another six months to live? You don't. So what are you waiting for?

!!! If you have a big 'YES, BUT...' in your mind now, pay attention to it and then put it on hold while you read on !!!

3. Life is short and you know it.

Whether you are going to live for another six days, six months, six or sixty years, life is short. Sometimes you are very keenly aware of this. For example, you probably become very conscious of your own mortality when you know, or hear of, someone who is terminally ill or who has died. You would probably have that acute awareness if you see or are involved in an accident, or have a serious injury, or physical or mental illness. You might become aware when you are watching a movie, or hearing a story, or reading a book that involves the topic (like right now).

When that happens, you most likely compare the things you do with the things that you would like to do. You might compare the things you have done with the things you would like to have done. For a while you are very motivated to spend more time and energy on the things that are of most value to you. You decide that, from now on, you'll devote more time to actually be with your loved ones instead of working all hours to take care of them. Now you'll get that book written, or spend time gardening, or travel to those countries you've always dreamed of visiting – or whatever is important to you.

And then, not long afterwards, your awareness of how short your life is fades from your conscious awareness. Your most valued people and ambitions drift away into the background again and you begin to live just the way you always have.

Now, the fact that you stop being so aware of your limited life span is not a completely bad thing. If you were thinking about it all the time you wouldn't be able to function effectively. You might give up on your goals and become unable to do anything at all because, 'What's the point if we're all going to die anyway?' On the other hand, you might take very rash actions without any care for the ongoing consequences. You might begin to make unrealistic demands on yourself and others; for example, to spend every moment of the day with each other just in case you or they will die soon. You might drift anxiously from one goal to another, always afraid you might die before you achieve the one big thing that would make your life worthwhile. If you had a 'YES, BUT...' thought earlier, it was probably about these kinds of concerns, and we'd agree with you. To think constantly about dying is no way to live.

However, here's our own 'YES, BUT...'

Not ever to think about it is no way to live either.

Generally people try not to think about the end of their life. It's a gloomy subject after all, and it can be frightening and depressing to focus on that reality. But even though it can be uncomfortable to anticipate the end of your life on a conscious level, we believe it is essential that you do that from time to time.

Why? Because out of sight is *not* out of mind.

Even if you aren't thinking about your own mortality at a conscious level, you will be aware of it at an unconscious level. At that level you always know that life is short. And, if you are not spending your precious short time on the things that are most important to you, you know that too. At that deep level you know that if you don't get started on the things that are meaningful and fulfilling to you, you may never get the chance. And this is a profound and continual source of stress.

4. To avoid this stress you must take control of your own life, even if that means risking the disapproval of others.

The stress we described above is caused by your sense that you are not in control *of your own life*. You want to do, think, say and feel certain things, and yet you feel pushed or compelled in some way by others to do, think, say and even feel something else. You feel that you are not free to plan and balance how you spend your life based on your own values and needs. Instead you feel driven to organize your life to fit in with the values and needs of other people. And all the time, at some level, you are aware that you don't have time for that.

In order to beat this stress you need to let go of your need for other people's approval and take control of your own life.

5. You also need to accept the limits of how much you can control.

We accept that if you knew for certain you had only a particular length of time to live that would give you the space to make drastic changes in the way you spend your time, and of course you would do that as soon as you realized that less important things are taking you away from the more important. And, we accept that you can't necessarily do that when your time span is less certain.

All we want to encourage you to do is to take control of how you balance your time between what is important to you and what is important to other people. Within the realistic limits of your personal or professional circumstances, do this in the way that is right according to your own values and wishes.

Of course it is fine to do things for other people. Sometimes you'll do it because you care about the person and it is important for you to do so, in which case it is one of your values. Sometimes you'll do it just because you want to and would enjoy doing it, in which case you are acting according to your own wishes.

Be there for others. Help and support them, and go along with what they want as much as you like. Just make sure that these are your decisions and you are the one who is in control.

CASE STUDY

Many years ago an acquaintance helped me with a difficulty I was having. I hadn't seen him for some time when I discovered he was in hospital recovering from a serious operation. I went to visit him, and when he returned home I continued to visit each week. When he became stronger we went out for a coffee or a walk each weekend. Then, I began to feel that this was too much for me. I needed more time at home to rest and be with my husband at weekends after travelling or working hard in the office during the week. I started to feel resentful of the time I spent with this acquaintance, so I began to arrange to see him less frequently. At first I felt bad about that. Then, after I thought about it, I stopped feeling bad. I care about him and he knows that. But, life is short, and I also care about myself and my husband. In fact, I care more about myself and my husband. I must make time for me and for us. My acquaintance and I now meet every month to six weeks or so and I'm happy to do that. We're becoming friends.

Don't wait for illness, injury or the suffering of others to push you to take control. Deliberately and consciously remind yourself from time to time of the unavoidable and inspirational truth. This is your own precious life, and it is very short. If that doesn't motivate you to begin to stand up to the influence of other people and live your own values, we don't know what will.

Taking control of your life

So now you're fired up and ready to take control of your own life. You're determined to live your life in a way that will be most fulfilling and satisfying to you, and according to your own values. Well done. Now how are you going to do it?

We believe that the most effective way forward is to develop and use the skills of EMPATHETIC ASSERTIVENESS.

What does that mean?

Empathetic

You probably have some idea already of what the word 'empathy' means.

To have empathy means to be able to understand another person's situation, motives and feelings. If you have a strong sense of empathy you can actually experience another person's emotions in your own body. So empathy leads you to laugh, or feel excited or tearful even when happy or sad events happen to someone else and not to you yourself. Often, you empathize because you have experienced something similar and can identify with their reactions. It isn't that you know or feel exactly what they are thinking or feeling because everyone reacts differently to things. But people's ability to have at least some sense of what others are going through is a key source of what we might call 'human connection', and it is a vital aspect of effective communication with others.

To be 'empathetic' just means to have the skill of empathy.

Assertiveness

You may also have an idea of what the word 'assertive' means. To be assertive is to be able to communicate your ideas, needs, wishes and intentions in a way that is clear and confident, and to do this without being hostile or over-demanding. This last aspect of assertiveness is crucial as a lot of people avoid expressing themselves assertively because they are afraid of coming across as uncaring or pushy.

Although we do want to encourage you to live by your own values, we want to be clear that we do not intend that you do this by acting without care or respect for others. Assertiveness is a combination of both strength and flexibility in relationships with other people.

We will explore the quality of assertiveness in some detail now since this is such an important aspect of the skill you need if you want to achieve KEY 2.

The quality of assertiveness

Exercise ten

People who are assertive show this in a number of ways that are both verbal (what they say) and non-verbal (how they say it, how they appear and what they do).

Before we describe these to you, have a go at listing them yourself. If you consider yourself to be assertive, then write down how you demonstrate that. Or perhaps you know or can think of a person whom you would describe as being assertive and write down what they do or how they communicate.

In each of the columns in the table below, write down 10 descriptions of how an assertive person would talk, look or behave.

Verbal assertive behaviour (what do assertive people communicate to others?)	Non-verbal assertive behaviour (how do assertive people talk, look and behave? eg voice, facial and body language, clothing and general appearance, etc)

Reflect

How was it for you to do that exercise? Did you find it easy or difficult?

Were you describing yourself? Most people find they can be assertive in some situations, but not all. Is that the case with you? Or do you struggle to be assertive at all?

Would you like to be able to communicate and behave more assertively more often?

Whenever we ask this question people say yes, they would like to be more assertive. You have probably answered the same.

Most people can see the attractiveness of the assertive approach. Those who are assertive seem to be able to be self-confident, self-assured and in control of their own lives without offending or alienating other people. In other words, they get what they want in life and other people still like them! Who wouldn't want to achieve that?

Now the final question. If you would like to be assertive and you realize that you are not, or not as often as you would like to be...

What's stopping you?

Even though people understand what it means to be assertive and recognize it when they see it they still find it very difficult to do themselves. Even when they've read self-help books and attended courses, etc they often still find that they are not able to put what they learn into practice. Why is it so difficult for people to be assertive, even when they know what it means and have learnt 'assertiveness skills'?

Remember the discussion about weight control we had in Chapter Six? There we said if you want to lose weight you need to stop asking 'how' because you already know the answer to that question – eat less and move around more. The question you need to ask is 'why' you are not doing those things even though you know you will achieve the weight loss you desire if you do. In other words, what's stopping you?

It's the same thing here. You know how to be assertive just as you know how to lose weight. If you are not convinced that you know how, take a look at our list below.

Verbal assertive behaviour (what do assertive people communicate to others?)	Non-verbal assertive behaviour (how do assertive people talk, look and behave? eg voice, facial and body language, clothing and general appearance etc)
State their own needs and priorities clearly	Voice steady, firm, middle-range tone, warm and sincere
Ask to be treated with respect	Not over-loud or quiet
Express their feelings	Clear and concise statements
Express their values and opinions	Facial expression matches their emotion
State clearly what they will and will not do	Keep eye contact and stay attentive while another person is speaking
Admit mistakes	Communicate directly with the source of their concern
Say if they don't understand	Upright and open posture, head held straight, eyes looking ahead
Ask for what they want	Clothing not brash or overly muted, and take care of their appearance
Ask questions to find out thoughts, feelings and needs of others	Open hand movements; face, neck and shoulder muscles relaxed
Actively listen	Relaxed and measured breathing, even when under pressure

Even though our list will not be exactly the same as yours and we'll have used different words and phrases, we are pretty sure that there will be a lot of similarities between your list and ours. You probably even have features on your list that you could add to ours.

So, you really do know how to be assertive.

Now you need to discover why you are not doing those things even though you know you will achieve your desired assertiveness if you do.

What stops you from being assertive?

When we ask our groups why they are not assertive even though they know how to be, they often say, 'It's easier said than done!'

As we've said earlier, we agree. It is easier said than done. In fact it can be very difficult indeed. We hope that by now you are already clear why. It's because, to be assertive, you have to act against your instincts. People find it difficult to be 'assertive' because they are driven by their instinctive needs either to be liked, or to be in control. If you are driven by either or both of these needs, you will not be able to be assertive.

The instinctive need to be liked leads people to be passive while the need to be in control leads them to be aggressive. Sometimes people are driven by both at the same time, leading them to be passive-aggressive. We'll take a look at each of these forms of behaviour to see how none of them will enable you to take control of your life while showing care and respect for others at the same time. In other words, how each of them stops you from being assertive.

1. Passive

People need to be liked

If you are driven by a need to be liked, you will not be able to fulfil the first requirement of assertiveness; that is 'to be able to communicate your ideas, needs, wishes and intentions in a way that is clear and confident' (to take control of your life). You might find it difficult to say in any way at all what you think and need, or will or won't do. If you feel that you must say something you will do it quietly, avoiding eye contact, and as though your view or wish is not nearly as important or valuable as those of other people. If someone asks you to repeat what you said, you'll say 'never mind, it was nothing'. You will say you agree whether you really agree or not. You will act to fulfil someone else's needs even if that goes against your own needs. You'll say you don't mind when you do. You'll say 'It's ok', when it isn't. When you make a statement you'll do it as though you were asking a question (voice rising at the end?). You might start (and end) with an apology, or use lots of '... um...'s and ... er...'s to try to soften your message. You will use your body language and clothing to make yourself as insignificant and unnoticeable as possible; you really want to just disappear into the background. You will put aside your own thoughts and feelings rather than risk losing the approval of others. We would call this behaviour 'passive'.

Do you recognize yourself here? Do you think that passive people suffer with stress? Of course they do. KEY 1 explained how and why that happens. People who need to be liked by everyone all the time are bound to suffer from stress because it is just not possible to achieve this. While you are trying to achieve the impossible you will become exhausted, perhaps even ill, and your resilience will be damaged and undermined.

2. Aggressive

People need to be in control

On the other hand, if you are driven by a need to be in control, you will be very well able to state your position clearly and confidently, but you will struggle to fulfil the second requirement of assertiveness; that is, able to do this 'without being hostile or over-demanding' (showing care and respect for others). You will be so afraid to lose control of any little bit of any aspect of your life or work that you will be compelled to overwhelm any challenge, contradiction or request for compromise. You need everything to be as you wish it to be. You need things to be done your way. You need other people to behave in ways that fit in with your beliefs and strategies for your own life. You are so afraid that you will have to compromise on your wishes and needs that you will state them in a way that makes it very difficult for other people to question or refuse you, and even to be honest about their own views and feelings.

You might do this, for example, by speaking loudly and fast and interrupting others. You might use your body language, eye contact and facial expressions to dismiss, overpower or threaten other people. You might say things like 'I don't care what you think, we're doing it this way', or 'It's my way or the highway!' You don't ask questions because you are not looking for answers from others. Whatever they think and whether they like it or not, you know what's right and that's how it's going to be. You need others to behave in ways that you believe are right and good for them in their own lives too. You often give advice or tell people what they 'should' or 'should not' do. Overall you are driven to impose your own will on other people to get them to comply with your needs and wishes. We would call this behaviour 'aggressive'.

Do you recognize yourself here? Do you think that people who are aggressive suffer from stress? Yes, of course. Again KEY 1 explained how and why. As with those who need approval, you are striving to achieve the impossible. It is simply not possible to control everything and everybody all of the time. If you try to do that you will become exhausted and ill, and you will weaken your resilience.

The illustrations above of passive and aggressive behaviour are, of course, extreme. Although there are some individuals whose behaviour matches these descriptions, most people fit one or other category much more loosely and in less obvious ways. Also, people are not usually only one or the other all the time. People find that in some situations or relationships they behave passively (for example in the presence of a dominant or authority figure such as a parent or manager) and more aggressively in others (for example with partners, children, friends or work colleagues). However, we would say that, in general, people have a stronger tendency towards one communication style. This will be the one that they fall back on when they are threatened or experiencing stress. In such a situation an individual's natural survival mechanism will become active and they will either fight aggressively to get their own way, or give in passively to avoid conflict, regardless of the particular relationship involved. If you were reluctant to put yourself into either extreme category earlier, would you be able to recognize yourself as 'tending to be passive' or 'tending to be aggressive', depending on the situation?

We should be clear that neither the passive nor the aggressive communication style is 'wrong' or 'bad' in itself. We would encourage you not to think about the way that you communicate in terms of 'right' or 'wrong'. Instead, ask yourself if the way that you approach or respond to another person is useful or helpful. There are some situations in which it would be a very good idea to communicate either passively or aggressively.

Can you think of a situation where it would be useful, or even essential to be very aggressive? Write it down here:

....

Can you think of a situation where it would be useful, or even essential to be very passive? Write it down here:

....

Now read on. We will come back to these questions shortly.

3. Passive-aggressive

People need to be both liked and in control at the same time

There is one more communication style that we need to look at. It's one that is far less commonly talked about, yet whenever we introduce this to our groups, most of the participants nod or even laugh in recognition. This is the 'passive-aggressive' style.

As you can see by the name, it is a combination of the passive and aggressive tendencies. We know that each of these on its own leads to stress. If you engage in behaviour that combines the two, then you are at even greater risk. Let's take a look at how the passive-aggressive style operates.

Imagine this everyday-life situation. You and your friend go to a Chinese restaurant for a meal. You would really have preferred the Italian. You've been looking forward to a pizza all day, but you don't say so. Instead you go to the Chinese, but you are disappointed and resentful. You show no interest in the menu and grudgingly choose something that you won't enjoy. You pick unenthusiastically at the food, barely respond to your friend's attempts at conversation and are generally sulky and sullen. It's clear to your friend that you are unhappy. They ask you what's wrong and you reply 'Nothing'. A little while later they ask if you are ok. You reply sharply, 'Yes, I'm fine.' Your friend can see that's not true, and they are aware of vague feelings of guilt. But they have no idea why you are unhappy or what they should be feeling guilty about. After all, you agreed to go to the Chinese – didn't you?

Or how about a situation where your partner has left dirty dishes in the sink again even though it's their turn to do the washing-up. You are angry, but instead of confronting your partner about this you tell them not to worry, you'll do it. Then you bang and crash around the kitchen and don't speak to them for the rest of the night. Your partner feels uncomfortable and guilty. But why should they be feeling guilty? You told them not to worry – didn't you?

Passive-aggressive behaviour is common in the workplace too. Imagine you've been finding your workload difficult for some time. There are many aspects of your job that seem to need immediate attention and you don't know where to start. You're feeling tired and irritable. You have a constant headache and are finding it difficult to stay focused and motivated. You've just received an e-mail from your manager telling you that they have been given new targets to meet and that you have to take on another piece of work to help them to meet those targets. You feel very anxious about this, so you decide to speak to your manager and let them know that you are struggling. When you get to your manager's office they address you over their shoulder while still reading and responding to e-mails on their computer screen. When you hesitate, they tell you to 'Carry on, I'm listening.'

How might a passive person react to this?

....

....

....

How might an aggressive person react?

....

....

....

Now that you've read a couple of illustrations of the passive-aggressive style, could you have a go at describing how a passive-aggressive person might respond?

....

....

....

If you look back at the descriptions of 'passive' and 'aggressive' you will be able to see that the passive person would probably just quietly give up and go back to their desk feeling hopeless and helpless. The aggressive person would more than likely shout at the manager, possibly swear, and storm out of the office. If you are passive-aggressive however, you would not directly challenge the manager's behaviour (passive) but would then leave the manager's office grumbling to yourself, and possibly others, about how 'The manager just doesn't care', and 'If they don't care why should I care?', and 'I'll do the #!?#! work for them but they needn't expect it to be any good!' (aggressive).

People who behave in this way do so because they are caught between equally powerful needs to be liked by other people and to be in control. They don't say directly what they actually think, need or want because they are afraid of losing approval. But then they feel frustrated and resentful because they feel themselves to have lost control. Once they give in to another person (passive) they still need to make some impact on the situation and perhaps even eventually get their own way. They do this by engaging in some form of punishing behaviour – such as sulking, rejecting, slamming doors, complaining to others, producing below-standard work, etc (aggressive). They hope the target of their resentment will somehow guess or realize what their true feelings or thoughts are and change their own behaviour accordingly. That way, the passive-aggressive person will have achieved control without the risk of loss of approval they fear would result if they were to refuse or openly ask for their needs and rights to be met.

CASE STUDY

In my story about meeting my acquaintance I said I had started to feel resentful of the time I spent with him. Still I kept arranging to visit each week because I was afraid he would think I was uncaring if I said I needed to meet less often. But I began to become irritable with him. Eventually I couldn't even greet him with a smile. The moment I decided to change was when I could tell he was confused and hurt by my abruptness. I realized I was causing him pain because of my combined fear of losing his approval and need to take control.

Of course my unpleasant behaviour was supposed to make him realize I was unhappy and to suggest himself that we should meet less often. That way I would get what I wanted without the risk of him thinking badly of me. But how was he to know what I was unhappy about? Why was that his responsibility? The only way we could meet comfortably was for me to risk his possible disappointment with me and tell him I needed to arrange to see him less frequently. He was fine about that. Why shouldn't he be? He cares about me too. I just wish I'd been assertive sooner. It would have made it easier for both of us.

The problem is that passive-aggressive behaviour very rarely works. People are unlikely to change their behaviour because they have been subjected to sulking and rejection, especially when they don't know why they are being punished in these ways. So the passive-aggressive person feels more and more powerless and frustrated, and becomes more and more stressed. If you are really honest with yourself you will probably be able to recognize that you sometimes behave in this way and can identify with how that feels.

Do you recognize yourself here? Do you think that people who are passive-aggressive suffer from stress? Absolutely. In fact, we would say that this form of behaviour is likely to be the most stress-inducing of all as it combines the damaging effects of both passiveness and aggression.

Equally, it is more than likely that you have been on the receiving end of passive-aggressive behaviour, and you know how difficult and uncomfortable that can be too. You know the passive-aggressive person wants something from you but you can't respond openly and honestly because the request isn't open and honest. You know the passive-aggressive person is unhappy or resentful but you don't know why because they agreed with you or said 'yes' to a request. So you feel confused and manipulated. Then, when the passive-aggressive person begins to punish you, you feel powerless. You know that you are being punished for something, but you don't know what that is so you can't do anything about it.

On the other hand, you might be very aware of the reason for the passive-aggressive's punishing behaviour. It's pretty clear when someone starts banging cupboard doors in the kitchen that they are punishing you for not doing the washing-up even though they said it was ok! However, although you know this, you don't want to accommodate them and appear to give in to what feels to you like manipulative and controlling behaviour. This leaves you in the unpleasant position of having achieved what you want but unable to take any pleasure or security in it because the passive-aggressive will act to undermine your enjoyment or sabotage your goals in some way.

All in all, we would have to say that passive-aggressive behaviour is the least useful and least constructive of all of the communication styles.

Earlier we asked you to think of a situation where it might be useful or even essential to be aggressive. Examples of this might be when people are in danger and you need them to act as you demand without question or argument: eg to stop a child who is about to put their hand on a hot cooker ring; to warn someone who is about to step into a road when there is traffic approaching; or to organize a fire evacuation, etc. In these situations, aggression will be the approach most likely to achieve a positive outcome.

We also asked you to think of a situation where it might be useful or even essential to be passive. Examples of this might be any situation where you or your loved ones would be in danger unless you comply with another person's requests or demands. In these situations it would probably be most constructive to respond passively.

When it comes to passive-aggressive communication, we would suggest that there is no situation where this would lead to the most positive or constructive outcome. It is painful and damaging to the individuals involved and destructive of relationships.

If you are aware that you behave in this way, we would strongly urge you to find a different way to ensure that your needs are met. When you become more assertive you won't need to demonstrate your needs and feelings in destructive and punishing ways because you will be able to state your position openly and honestly.

Also, if you recognize that there are times when you are on the receiving end of passive-aggression, then you need to be able to interrupt the manipulative agreement-punishment cycle. Again, assertiveness is the way. When you are more assertive you will be able to challenge the initial passiveness. You'll be able to let the passive-aggressive person know that you are aware that there is a mismatch between what they are saying and how they actually seem to feel, and that you'd really prefer them to be honest with you.

Which brings us back to EMPATHETIC ASSERTIVENESS.

The skills and qualities of empathetic assertiveness

As we've said, we believe that the most effective way to take control and to live your values according to KEY 2 is to develop and use the skills of empathetic assertiveness.

Let's have a quick recap of what that means.

Empathetic

We said that to have empathy means to be able to understand, or have a sense of, another person's situation, motives and feelings. To be empathetic just means 'to have the skill of empathy'.

Assertiveness

We said that to be assertive is to be able to communicate your ideas, needs, wishes and intentions in a way that is clear and confident, and to do this without being hostile or over-demanding.

So 'empathetic assertiveness' simply means:

To be able to take control of your own life and live according to your own wishes, needs and values, while always taking into account the wishes, needs and values of others.

We hope you can now see clearly why you will only be able to achieve this ability if you can let go of your need for approval, control or both. Now, we want to introduce you to a concept that is at the core of this KEY, and that might give you more courage and commitment to let these powerful drivers go and act more assertively more often.

That is the concept of 'rights'.

Assertiveness and rights

You have a right to determine your own life

People who are assertive recognize that it is very important to determine their own lives. In fact, they believe it is so important that they regard this as a 'right'.

They believe that they have a right to determine their own life because they are aware that life is terribly short, and that once it is over they won't get another chance to do it the way that they want to do it.

> Of course there are people who believe that the life they are living now isn't their only chance and that they will be reincarnated into another life at another time. However, there would be few who would argue that it would be possible to have this life again; in this place and time, and with these people. You won't get a chance to do this life again.

So, assertive people are prepared to risk the disapproval of others sometimes to ensure that they themselves are ultimately in control of something as precious as their own life.

BUT, they don't just see this as a right that they have, they see it as a right that all human beings have. Everyone has an equal right to determine their own lives because their lives are also short and equally precious to them.

So assertive people are willing to let go of their need to be in control of other people, and give others an equal chance to determine their own lives too.

We could express this as an assertiveness motto:

Your rights are equal to, not less or more than, the rights of any other person.

If you take a look back at the table that we completed for Exercise Ten you'll find that we described assertive people as being able to:

- state their own needs and priorities clearly;
- ask to be treated with respect;
- express their feelings;
- express their values and opinions;
- state clearly what they will and will not do;
- admit mistakes;
- say if they don't understand;
- ask for what they want.

They feel able to do these things, without apology, because they believe they have a right to do so. Crucially, though, the assertive person believes that everyone else has an equal right to do the same.

Once you adopt this position you will be able to allow yourself to behave assertively safe in the knowledge that this need not mean, and indeed shouldn't mean, that you become selfish and uncaring. Quite the opposite. When you become assertive you demonstrate real care and respect for others because you give them the permission and opportunity to be assertive too. You let them take control of their own lives. This could be the greatest gift you ever give to another person.

Developing the skills of empathetic assertiveness

We've been talking a lot about communication. However, this book is about building resilience. We introduce the concept of empathetic assertiveness into our KEYS because we know how stress can arise through lack of assertiveness and the damage that stress can do to a person's resilience. You need to work to develop the skills of empathetic assertiveness so you can protect yourself from stress and maintain your own personal resilience.

Although we have presented some ideas on the qualities and skills involved in behaving assertively, unfortunately we don't have space in this book to go into these in very specific detail. That's another course and a different book. If you've realized through reading this chapter that you need to learn more about how to become assertive, then we would recommend you take a look at some of the books from our reading list, or find a course or workshop that you can attend. Assertiveness skills can be so powerful and life-transforming that it would be well worth the effort.

Having said that, we would like to give you our top tip for assertive communication to get you started.

Top tip for behaving assertively: use empathy first

Before you make any assertive statement about yourself, put yourself in the other person's shoes and say something that you sense or know about them. With this approach you will find it much easier to do the things that you might find most difficult, such as challenging someone else's behaviour and saying 'no'. It will be easier for you because once the other person feels that their position has been respected they will be able to accept yours more readily and easily.

Always start with something about the other person = 'you':

'I can see/hear/sense/understand what <u>you</u> say/feel/think/need...

Then say what you need to say about yourself = 'I':

However, I feel/think/need...'

Let's take a look at a few examples of how this might work in practice. We've underlined the empathetic 'you' response and the assertive 'I' message.

1. Challenging someone else's passive or passive-aggressive behaviour

'I know <u>you sometimes find it difficult to say what you want</u>, and although you've agreed to... I can see you're not very happy about it. <u>I'd really prefer</u> it if you could tell me what you really want, then I'll know where I stand and there'll be no bad feelings between us. Ok?'

'Maybe you're telling me nothing's wrong because <u>you don't want to upset me or cause an argument</u>. Only, the thing is, I can tell that you're angry/unhappy/anxious and <u>I'd honestly prefer to know</u> what's troubling you.'

'You're telling me you don't mind if I do/don't do... and I think that might be because <u>you don't want to put pressure on me</u>. I can hear from your voice though that you really do mind. Please tell me how you really feel and <u>I'll be honest about what I can and can't do</u>.'

All of these examples demonstrate assertiveness on your part, and also empower the other person to abandon their passive or passive-aggressive approach and become more honest with you too.

2. Challenging unacceptable behaviour

From our earlier example about the encounter with the manager:

'I see that <u>you are very busy</u> and would like to be able to listen to me while you are doing something else. However, I have come to see you about something that is <u>very important to me</u> and <u>I need your full attention</u>.'

3. Challenging someone who is being aggressive or abusive

'I can see that <u>you are very angry/upset</u> and I do understand your reasons for that. However, <u>I would appreciate</u> it if you could approach me in a more respectful way.'

'What <u>you're saying is important</u> and I want to know about what's bothering you. However <u>I must ask you not to become personally abusive</u>.'

NB We avoided the word 'BUT' in these examples. That's because the word 'but' can seem to cancel out the empathetic message you've just been so careful to put across.

Of course, you will use words and expressions that suit you and feel comfortable for you to say. What you say and how you say it will also depend on the situation. As long as you get the idea, and can truly let go of needing to be liked and in control, then you will find this comes more and more naturally over time.

4. Saying 'no'

This is the biggest challenge for people with both passive and aggressive tendencies. Passive people struggle to say 'no' at all, while those who are aggressive say it in such a dismissive and rejecting manner that they undermine or alienate the person making the request.

When you use empathy first you will be able to say 'no' with such grace that, while the other person might feel disappointed, they will still feel respected rather than rejected. In turn they will respect you too, even though they are being declined by you. To achieve this, you:

1 thank them for making the request to you;
2 use empathy to be clear that you recognize the importance *to them* of what they need (even though it might seem trivial or unimportant to you);
3 show them that you take their choice to ask you as a compliment (if appropriate);
4 decline the request.

It might sound something like this;

> 'Thank you for asking me to help you with that, it's clearly something <u>that's important to you</u> and I'm flattered/honoured/pleased that you should choose to approach me. <u>Unfortunately I'm not able to at the moment</u> as I already have too much to do myself. Thanks again for asking though. Perhaps I could help another time.'

If it doesn't seem appropriate to use number 3, it would be like this:

> 'Thank you for asking me to help you with that, it's clearly something <u>that's important to you. Unfortunately, I'm not able to at the moment</u> as I already have too much to do myself. Thanks again for asking though. Perhaps I could help another time.'

Sometimes you need to say 'no' *unless something changes*. This is more of a negotiation than an outright refusal. For example, back to that encounter with the manager (when they've started to pay attention!) you might say:

> 'Thanks for letting me know about this. I understand <u>how important it is</u> and I appreciate that you think I can handle it. However, <u>I already have a number of things</u> that seem to need immediate attention, so <u>I'm afraid I will not be able to</u> help you <u>unless</u> you can help me re-prioritize my current workload.'

Or, you could say it more positively:

> 'Thanks for letting me know about this. I understand <u>how important it is</u> and I appreciate that you think I can handle it. However, <u>I already have a number</u>

of things that seem to need immediate attention, so I will only be able to help if you can help me re-prioritize my current workload.'

You will use your own words of course, and the content will depend on the specific context and request. But, in any case, the key is to express respect and empathy for the person even though you are refusing the request.

Final notes about saying 'no'

1. Notice that there are two words absent from our examples.
One is the word 'no' itself. As a general rule, a refusal is likely to be more easily received if you can avoid a blunt response like *'No, I can't/won't...'*

Also absent is the word 'sorry'. You want to say 'sorry' to show that you have empathy for the other person's disappointment and to avoid losing their approval. However, there is no need to apologize because you are not doing anything wrong. You are not doing anything wrong because you have a right to say 'no' and 'yes' according to your own values. You can show your empathy more assertively by saying things like *'Unfortunately...'*, or *'Sadly...'*, or *'I'm afraid that...'*, or *'I wish I could because I can see how much you need/how important this is... however, unfortunately...'* etc.

Stephen Covey put it like this, 'You have to decide what your highest priorities are and have the courage – pleasantly, smilingly, non-apologetically, to say "no" to other things. And the way you do that is by having a bigger "yes" burning inside.'

We believe the 'bigger "yes" burning inside' is to yourself and your own needs and values.

2. Once you have stated your position, stick to it. People might try to change your mind with persuasion and even manipulation. Resist this and be firm with your boundaries and about what you need. Simply reinforce your empathy for the other person's needs, and then repeat your response as many times as necessary.

3. As an assertive person you will always remember that everyone else has the same right to say 'no' and 'yes' according to their own values. If you make a request and the other person refuses, avoid trying to persuade or argue them into it, or to question them about why they won't do it. Just say, 'OK, no problem'. If they say 'Sorry...' tell them there is no need to apologize. This is not passive. It is the recognition that they have the same 'bigger "yes" burning inside'. It is truly powerful and empowering empathetic assertiveness in action.

We hope that these few examples have inspired you to begin to try out some assertive approaches and possibly to find out more. It's not easy, but we promise it will get easier the more often you do it. Find your own style of assertive expression. Stand up for your own rights. Start to do it now.

KEY 3   SUMMARY

You have a right to determine your own life

- Life is short and if you don't get started on the things that are meaningful and important to you, you may never get the chance.

- To take control of your own life, develop empathetic assertiveness. This is the ability to live according to your personal needs and values, while taking into account the needs and values of others.

- To be assertive you need to let go of your needs to be in control and to be liked. If you need control, you are in danger of behaving aggressively. If you need to be liked you are in danger of being passive.

- If you accept that everyone, including yourself, has the right to live according to their own values then you will be able to behave assertively without appearing selfish, uncaring or aggressive.

If you don't have a plan for your life, someone else does.
ANTHONY ROBBINS

KEY 4

09

Change is the only constant

People fear change because they fear the unpredictable. But the reality is that change is inevitable in life and you need to be able to respond positively and flexibly to the unexpected.

In Part One we asked you to write down 10 aspects of life that you believe could lead a person to become stressed. We also provided a list of potential stressors from samples of our live groups' responses. Our list contained the following:

- insecurity, threat of redundancy;
- beginnings and endings;
- divorce;
- moving house;
- bereavement.

We would say that the reason people find these kinds of events stressful is that they all involve a strong element of *change*. Are there any items in your list that would fit into this category?

In fact, in our list 'frequent change' appears as a stressor in its own right. Have you written 'change' in your list too?

We would be surprised if there were no items in your list related to change, possibly including the word 'change' itself. That's because human beings are programmed to fear change.

Change threatens people's need for control

The psychological driver underlying people's fear of change is their instinctive need to be in control. Remember, in KEY 1, we said that being in control would have been essential for survival thousands of years ago. At that time humans would have needed to be able to sense tiny changes in temperature, sound, smell and movement around them. They would have been so finely tuned to all aspects of their environment that they would have been able to identify what kind of danger these might have indicated. Fuelled by the brain's short route fight-or-flight response, they could then have taken appropriate, rapid evasive action to make themselves and their tribe safe.

So, our evolutionary ancestors were change-averse because change very often indicated real threats to their survival. Change equalled danger. They needed to have, and actually had, a great deal of control over their environment. This enabled them to be able to escape or fight off those threats.

In our modern place and time, changes are more complex and frequent. They are much less physical and predictable, and the consequences are much less certain. Therefore it simply isn't possible for people now to have the same level of control over change. And, that's ok. Nowadays people don't need to have that degree of physical control because change very rarely indicates a real threat to survival. Yet, people still have the same instinctive need to have that control.

This leads them to have the same fight-or-flight response, not only to change itself, but even to the slightest sense of the possibility of change – even though there is no real threat to their survival. Why? What is it about change that threatens people's sense of having control so much that it triggers their survival mechanism, even when there is no physical threat to their life?

We gave you the answer to that question in our definition of 'stress' in Part One. There we said:

> As far as your instinct for survival is concerned, being unable to cope is as much a threat to your life as a physical attack would be, and that instinct for survival reacts in the same way to both – with the fight-or-flight response.

When people know what is going to happen in their lives and can predict the consequences, then they can prepare to deal with those so they can keep themselves and their loved ones safe. That gives them a sense of being able to cope. But, most often when things change, elements of both the unknown and the unpredictable are introduced into a person's life. People cannot control things they don't know and can't predict. So change can easily trigger a sudden, deep sense of being unable to cope. This is the short route fear response, which is the very definition of stress.

These days change is inevitable and frequent. So to respond to it with an instinctive fear that you won't be able to cope can become a source of chronic stress and seriously undermine your resilience. If you tend to be fearful or resistant to change, you need to develop a different way to react to this ever-present aspect of daily life.

How do you react to change?

Exercise eleven

Whether you like it or not, life is constantly changing. Ask yourself how you feel about recent changes that now affect everyone. For example:

- ever-expanding electronic and instantaneous communication;
- growing dependence on technology and power supply;
- no more reliance on a 'job for life';
- advances in genetic engineering.

Now add to those a list of some changes that are more immediate and specific to you personally. Identify three or four aspects of your life that are changing, or that you anticipate will change in the near future:

-
-
-
-
-

In a year's time your life will be different from the way it is now. Perhaps it will be different in the ways you've identified above, or perhaps in ways you cannot yet anticipate. Reflect for a moment or two on that realization. Then look at the list of words in the table below. Ignore the Ds and Os in column 3 for now. In column 2, put a tick in the boxes against all the words that reflect the way you feel overall about your changing life. Leave the boxes blank where the words do not reflect your reactions. Be honest!

1	2	3
anxious	☐	D
flexible	☐	O
critical	☐	D
enthusiastic	☐	O
obstructive	☐	D
fearful	☐	D
curious	☐	O
humourless	☐	D
organized	☐	O
aggressive	☐	D
focused	☐	O
interested	☐	O
frustrated	☐	D
hopeful	☐	O
moody	☐	D
happy	☐	O
angry	☐	D
optimistic	☐	O
pessimistic	☐	D
positive	☐	O
excited	☐	O
helpless	☐	D
negative	☐	D
proactive	☐	O
welcoming	☐	O
withdrawn	☐	D

Now you will see that each of your ticks is in a box alongside a D or an O.

We know it's a very simplistic test. However, whether you have ticked more boxes by a D or an O will give an impression of how you currently respond to change. Count the number of boxes you ticked by each and write the numbers down here:

How many by D? ...

How many by O? ...

Is your reaction to change mostly D or O?

Reflect

The classifications of D- and O-types were created by change expert Daryl Conner and introduced in his book, *Managing at The Speed of Change*. They are designed to indicate your innate response to change.

D-type

The D-type response is the instinctive reaction that perceives change as DANGER. It is the 'Can't cope!' stress response that is triggered by a person's sense of loss of control. This happens because change brings with it fear of the unknown. If you don't know what's happening or going to happen, how do you prepare for or avoid threats to your survival? Very often, people who have this response make it worse by imagining all the terrible things that change will bring (we talked about this in KEY 1). Each time they do this their 'Can't cope!' reaction is triggered again. The result is chronic stress.

As a result D-type reactions are often like this:

- Anxious
- Critical
- Fearful
- Humourless
- Frustrated
- Angry
- Pessimistic
- Helpless.

So the D-type approach to change is likely to be:

- Obstructive
- Moody
- Negative
- Aggressive
- Withdrawn.

O-type

Some people have the ability to overcome the instinctive D-type response and replace it with the O-type reaction. When O-type people encounter change, instead of danger, they perceive OPPORTUNITY.

It is human instinct to react to change with the fight-or-flight stress reaction. So everyone will react that way; you can't help it. In Part One we said:

> You can't stop the short route firing when it perceives a psychological threat in a particular situation. That is instinctive and unconscious, and you can't control something that is outside of your conscious awareness.

But then we said:

> What you can do is gradually teach your brain what is and what isn't worth being afraid of until the short route begins to fire less and less often.

This is what people who have an O-type reaction to change are able to do. How do they do this? Well, remember the instinctive short route reaction operates without using the thinking part of the brain that can analyse a situation and work out the most appropriate response. O-type people overcome their instinctive fear reaction to change by engaging the long route in the brain and giving themselves time to think.

Instead of allowing the short route to fire over and over again, O-type people use their long route thinking brain to tell themselves they will be able to cope and they will survive, even though the change might have come out of the blue and might not be something they have chosen. They have their own version of 'Don't Kill George!' (remember from KEY 1?). When faced with the unknown they don't increase their stress by imagining the worst. Instead they accept the 'not knowing' for the present and believe that, when they do know, they'll deal with it.

They may go even further and recognize that the change might bring some benefit. They may think something like, 'This is not a change that I would have chosen, and there might be difficulties to overcome, but there will be something in it for me too. In some way I can turn this into an opportunity to have new experiences and to grow.' It isn't that they expect the change to deliver opportunity on a plate. They expect themselves to make that happen.

This leads O-type reactions to be more like this:

- Enthusiastic
- Curious
- Interested
- Hopeful
- Happy
- Optimistic
- Excited
- Welcoming.

So the O-type approach to change is:

- Flexible
- Focused
- Positive
- Organized
- Proactive.

Of the D- and O-type responses, which do you think will lead to a less stressful and more constructive approach to change? Obviously, the O-type.

D-type reactions to change give rise to stress, and stress undermines your ability to be resilient. You'll know from the definitions we gave in Part One that the crucial quality of resilience is flexibility. It is in the area of change management that flexibility is a key quality to develop – and there it is at the top of the list of O-type approaches. There is no escaping the reality that change is constant and often inevitable in life. So if you discovered in the last exercise that you have a tendency to be D-type in your reactions to change, it is well worth cultivating O-type qualities if you want to build and maintain the flexibility that is at the heart of your resilience.

It is really important to recognize that sometimes change can bring real threats that do in fact challenge your ability to cope. If that's the case, your thinking brain will tell you so. If the change is risky and not inevitable you are perfectly entitled to use your intelligence and energy to oppose or avoid it. If the change is risky and inevitable then your fear will motivate you to seek support and help. The problem arises when your reactions are simply instinctive and habitual and you react with fear when there is no need to be afraid.

The reality is that most of the time people do cope. Often they thrive, even when change is massive and initially unpleasant. How many times have you heard someone say they found redundancy/divorce/relocation, etc very difficult and even traumatic at first, but then declare 'it was the best thing that could have happened to me!'? Have you ever discovered that for yourself?

Learning to be an O-type

First let's remind you that O-type people have the same instinctive response to change as everyone else. In the fraction of a second it takes the short route to fire they will experience an instant of fear too. As we said in Part One, your body is well adapted to recover from this kind of infrequent acute stress. It is when this is allowed to continue or happen repeatedly that the effects begin to undermine your physical and mental well-being.

There is just one difference between the O- and the D-type. The D-type allows the fear response to keep firing and even encourages it by imagining catastrophic events and consequences. On the other hand, the O-type interrupts the fear response. They do this by making a conscious decision to take some time to think. They analyse what is happening and then decide what action to take based on their observations and self-awareness.

In a nutshell, to become an O-type you need to take time to consciously think carefully about the situation. This means:

1 Remind yourself that change brings opportunities as well as challenges, and look for the good news.

2 Make a plan.

We'll look at the techniques and strategies involved in these now.

The O-type in action

1. Look for the good news

When people seek out or imagine negative aspects of change and exaggerate those, they fail to see the potential and the opportunity that the change can bring. The next exercise will show you the process that an O-type goes through to counter that instinctive D-type response.

An accomplished O-type will do this exercise in their head. It is such a habit for them to react to change in this way that it becomes almost automatic. They may not even be aware of the effort it takes for them to do this. It does take effort though, because the instinct is to do the opposite; to focus on the threats and not the good news. So if you are used to following that instinct and notice only what is difficult and frightening about change then you will have to make a real effort to break this habit. If you are not used to looking for opportunity in change it will be more effective to write it down to begin with. If you keep practising this strategy it will become easier and more natural. Eventually you'll do it automatically too.

Exercise twelve

Just for the moment we will allow you to wallow in pessimism. In the left-hand column in Table 1 below, write down any events involving change that you are currently dealing with, or think you might encounter over the next year or so. In the right-hand column, note why these are difficult for you. What are you anxious about? What are you afraid you will lose?

TABLE 1

Anxieties about current and future changes in my life		
	Describe the change	What is it about this change that makes me anxious or afraid? What could I lose?
1		
2		
3		
4		

Now, re-enter the same changes in the left-hand column in Table 2 below. This time, in the right-hand column write down why each of these changes is good news. What opportunities do these changes potentially open up for you? What can you be excited about gaining from them?

There are two rules for this part of the exercise:

1 You must put at least one thing in the right-hand column for each entry on the left.

and

2 What you put in the right-hand column must be a real potential opportunity or gain.

It is very important that your entries in the right-hand column are not mindless fabrications. If they are, your brain will simply reject them and the negative impressions will remain the most powerful. You need the positive ideas to be at least as powerful, if not more so, than the negative. That will only happen if they are believable to you. Don't worry if you find this challenging. We've already said it takes effort at first to break instinctive habits. Stick with it and don't move on till you can follow those two rules.

TABLE 2

	Potential opportunities to look forward to in the changes in my life	
	Describe the change	What is it about this change that I could be excited about and look forward to? What could I gain?
1		
2		
3		
4		

Reflect

First, what was it like for you to do that exercise? Was it easier to complete the right-hand column in Table 1 or 2? If you had more O-type ticks in the previous exercise, you probably found it quite easy to complete both tables, though possibly more easy to do the second. If you had a lot of D-type ticks in your table in the previous exercise, you probably found it easy to complete the first table and more difficult to do that for the second. If you found table 2 hard to finish we would like to reassure you again that this will get easier with practice. The next of our 7 KEYS will help with this too.

Second, if you have tended towards D-type reactions to current and anticipated changes in your life and yet managed to complete the right-hand column, how do you feel now about those changes? Write down your feelings here:

....

....

....

We do this exercise frequently with groups when we are asked to help with change management in organizations. We usually begin by going round the individuals in the group to ask how the changes at work will affect them and how they feel about that. In all the years we have been doing this job it has never, and we mean never, been the case that someone has started by telling us about the possible opportunities. People always begin with their fears and anxieties. We are not very surprised at this because we understand human beings tend instinctively towards D-type reactions to change.

So, we start by getting them to put all of their concerns down on a large piece of paper. They have no difficulty doing this. They get everything off their chests about what they are afraid of, what they'll lose and what makes them angry or frustrated. Quite often people complain about lack of information. They don't know exactly what will happen and when. So, although sometimes the things they are afraid of and angry about are real, often they are reacting to things they've made up. For example, people don't know whether or not they will be made redundant, but they're already feeling and behaving as though:

1 it is a definite outcome;

and

2 it is a complete catastrophe.

Having worked with us in this book up till now, you will be able to predict our approach to this. Think about it before you read on. How do you think we would approach a group of people who are reacting to change like this?

Ok, now we'll tell you...

We begin by talking about the need for control and how important it is to accept 'not knowing' instead of making something up and 'killing George'. Then we ask them to do the same exercise you've just completed. We ask them to write down why all the changes they are concerned about are actually good news. It takes them a while to get started on this and they spend some moments looking at each other with puzzled expressions on their faces. But then, they do it. They begin to fill their paper with potential gains and opportunities they hadn't thought of before.

Now we begin to notice a transformation. At the start they will have been serious, defensive, and sometimes even upset and tearful. By the end of the exercise, even though nothing is actually different about the situation itself, they are lively, chatty and often laughing and joking with each other. This reflects a powerful shift in their response to what is happening to them. When we ask how they feel they say things like cheered, uplifted, energized and more confident. They say they feel hopeful, and sometimes even enthusiastic and excited.

We hope you experienced something like that when you finished this exercise.

The important thing to remember is that we are not advising an unrealistically over-optimistic 'Pollyanna' approach that ignores the challenges and losses that change can bring with it. You need to pay attention to those so you can deal with them appropriately. All we are advising is that you balance this with the recognition that, as well as challenge, change always brings opportunities too. Your task is to look for these. Look for the ways in which the changes you face will enable you to grow, to diversify and to have experiences that will ultimately enrich and strengthen you. If you think about it, it is only when something changes that the opportunity for this kind of personal growth and development arises. So maybe instead of fearfully avoiding change, people should seek it out and make it happen themselves!

The O-type in action

2. Make a plan

You've seen how to develop a more realistically optimistic approach to change, and we hope you can also see how this will help you to build the flexible resilience you need to be able to handle change more effectively. That flexibility will enable you to feel that you can be more in control of events and so will reduce any unnecessary stress. To take control in a practical way, you need to focus on what you do know about what is happening or likely to happen and make a plan of action that will protect you and others in your care. To ensure the best outcome for your plan you need to:

1 Be clear about the end-point.

2 Break it down and celebrate achievements along the way.

3 Be prepared for setbacks.

4 Seek support.

Making a plan

i. Be clear about the end-point

In KEY 2 we encouraged you to become clear about the goals you have for your life. This goal clarity will serve you well when you embark on a process of change. When you make a plan for change begin with the outcome you desire in mind. Ask yourself, 'What do I want to achieve, and how can the change that is occurring now, or about to occur, assist in delivering that result?'

We cannot be prescriptive about this for you. It is for you, and only you, to say what is an important goal. However, here are some guidelines to give a flavour of how you might approach particular changes. For example:

If you are handling loss of a job, be clear about the opportunity this creates for finding a better job, the right job, in the future. Use this time to clarify what you really want to do, where you'd like to work and what sort of people you'd like to work with.

If you are having to relocate, focus on what you would like to get out of the move. What opportunities does the new area offer for you to continue with the activities you enjoy and value? Does it offer facilities that would enable you to embark on new adventures? How will you meet people and make new friends? Have a vision of your new life as you want it to be.

If you are separating from a partner, decide if you want a new relationship and, if you do, what you want from a new relationship. Recognize how the separation will help you to create a more fulfilling and happier future.

If you suffer injury or illness, focus on the things you can do rather than what you can't do, and on what you will be able to do in time. Envisage the new skills and interests you will develop as a result of the change in your physical abilities.

When you are thinking about your end-point for a plan to deal with any of these kinds of changes, think further ahead than the next six months or year. The period immediately following a big change can be full of both practical and emotional upheaval, so it might be difficult to envisage achieving a goal within that time and you could become discouraged. Think about what you want in the next 5, 10 or even 15 years. That will help to keep your thinking on track in the early days.

We're not suggesting that this should be easy and some changes will be more difficult than others to deal with in this way. But, the change has happened or will happen anyway, and you have no option other than to accommodate it somehow or other. We can assure you that a clear vision of possible opportunities in any kind of change will see you through.

CASE STUDY

I read a magazine article about a man who had a stroke. As a result of a blood clot at the base of his brain he also developed a rare neurological disorder called 'locked-in' syndrome. He was not expected to recover. The prognosis was 'either death or living death'. But he had a vision, a vision of recovery, and he began to work towards that. He focused on achieving that great goal one small step at a time (as we described in KEY 2). He worked on swallowing, then on moving his head. He began to communicate by blinking while he concentrated on learning to speak. Gradually, amazingly, he did recover. Sixteen years after the stroke he says, 'I do things I was never able to before... I'm a softer, kinder person now, and I have new friends and more interests. In many ways I feel more alive than I ever did before my stroke.'

('I was locked in my own body', Experience, *The Guardian* Weekend, 23 Oct 2010)

Of course, this is an extreme example. We wouldn't like you to imagine we are suggesting that this should, or even could, be easy, or that someone would have failed in some way if they were unable to achieve this kind of outcome for themselves. Each individual has their own unique experience of illness or injury, with their own unique set of challenges and obstacles. It's just one man's story that illustrates the potential power of this aspect of O-type behaviour.

Making a plan

ii. Break it down and celebrate achievements along the way

Change takes time and it can be easy to get downhearted about the length and the difficulty of the journey. To overcome this, set some markers along the way and decide on celebrations or personal rewards that you can look forward to.

The breakdown into discrete steps can be quite a complex process when you are planning for a big change. It can help to create a written timetable to keep you on track. For example, you might use a table like the one below, which is called a Gantt chart (named after Henry Gantt who designed the chart in around 1910–15). This is a bar chart in which the various steps are recorded showing where each step will start and finish and the length of time each step will take – often with overlapping times. Here is a Gantt chart we created for someone planning for redundancy in 'week 4'.

	week 1	week 2	week 3	week 4	week 5	week 6	week 7	week 8	week 9	week 10
Chill out & reflection time	▓				▓					
Obtain references from employer		▓	▓							
Work with recruitment consultant		▓	▓							
Revise CV		▓								
Research best source of job adverts			▓	▓						
Rehearse interview skills						▓				
Send job applications			▓	▓		▓	▓			
Be available for interview						▓	▓	▓	▓	▓

The Gantt chart enables you to see what you have to be doing and when. Each of these stages is a milestone along the way and each justifies acknow-ledgement and celebration. Maybe you'll have a drink with friends or a day out, or just a lazy evening in; whatever you will really enjoy and will let you feel good about yourself.

Notice that 'Chill out & reflection time' is a stage in its own right. This is essential to give yourself the chance to engage your 'thinking brain' and over-come needless fear. As we've said, this can be a real effort because it goes against your instinct. Your instinct is to fight or run, not chill and reflect. If you can spend a whole week resisting the fight-or-flight reaction and instead stop, think, focus on goals and opportunities and make a plan, you deserve a reward!

Making a plan

iii. Be prepared for setbacks

During a change programme there is sometimes a period of time when things seem to start getting worse before they get better. This is often called the 'implementation dip'. When this happens it can be easy to lose heart and give up.

Change takes you into uncharted territory and it would be surprising if it delivered a smooth ride all the way. The 'implementation dip' is a common part of a change process and is not an indication of any incompetence, or lack of energy and commitment on your part. If you find yourself in one of these dips, recognize it for what it is and don't let it dishearten you.

CASE STUDY

I was in a safe, well-paid job-for-life. However, I had gone as far as possible within that organization and the job was no longer stimulating and fulfilling. So I took one of the most courageous steps of my life. I resigned, secured the financial support of some investors and set up a new business in a field that particularly interested me. After the excitement of the start-up things got decidedly worse. We failed to attract clients as we had anticipated, and the investors expressed their displeasure that their money was not delivering what they had expected. I felt anxious, and missed the secure comfort of my old life. One day I heard the psychiatrist Dr Anthony Clare talking on the radio. He was saying he had spent time with a lot of people towards the end of their lives and found that they rarely regretted the chances they had taken, even if they had not succeeded. They regretted the things they had *not* done. Dr Clare's advice was 'if you have an opportunity in life, even if it entails risk and setback, then take it'. I gritted my teeth through the difficulties of the early days, and the business became successful.

Bear in mind that things change all the time and there is no reason to suppose the world will stand still while you systematically go through the steps of your plan. Remember the key quality of resilience is flexibility. It is useful to create a timetable; however, be prepared to respond to the unexpected over that period. You may need to adjust your timings. You may even need to adapt your goal to a different set of circumstances. Adjust and adapt as you need. Just make sure you always have a goal in mind and that you are travelling towards it.

Making a plan

iv. Seek support

Your brain's primitive short route will fire whenever there is a perception that you won't be able to cope. We believe that perception will most often be wrong. We believe that if people give themselves time to think things through, most of the time they will realize they can, in fact, cope. That's why we've been encouraging you to counter the instinctive fear reaction to change and to adopt the strategies we've outlined in this chapter.

But there are times when the primitive brain reacts to a 'Can't cope!' perception and it will be right; you truly can't cope. Sometimes a change can be so overwhelming that it is actually more than you can handle. Your thinking brain agrees with your primitive brain that there is real reason to be afraid. Even when you realize this there is no need to respond by letting your fight-or-flight mechanism keep on firing and raising your stress levels. You don't have to go it alone. Get help. Overcome your primitive fear so you can engage your thinking brain to work out what kind of help you need, who will be the best person (or people) to provide that help, and how you will go about asking for it.

In our definitions at the start of this book we compared 'resilience' to 'strength'. People who are strong, or want to appear strong or perfect (recognize 'need for approval', KEY 1?) are reluctant to ask for help because they are afraid this will mean they are weak or will seem to be weak. They don't have the flexibility to adapt their approach, so they keep their fears and needs to themselves and tough it out alone. But, remember what we said in our definitions? A strong person is like a rock that can be chipped or even broken and cannot put itself back together again. This is not what we want for you.

Aim instead for resilience. As a resilient person you have the flexibility to shift your approach to suit the needs of a situation. So you can deal with things alone when that's appropriate and ask others for support if that's what is required to see you through. This flexibility means you won't break because you can allow yourself to bend with pressure. You bend by letting go of your need for approval and to be perfect (KEY 1) and by showing how you feel and asking for what you need (empathetic assertiveness, KEY 3).

So make other people part of your change plan. Family and friends can provide practical and moral support, and can cheer you along. Strong people don't cry, resilient people most certainly do. Those closest to you can provide a shoulder for that purpose. Colleagues and professional contacts can be a great help too. They can contribute the benefit of their own experience and expertise and provide practical assistance also.

> Often the development of relationships is an activity that sits in the Important and Not Urgent quadrant of the matrix we introduced in KEY 2. You know relationships are important and you value them, but the urgent busyness of everyday life gets in the way. You need to deliberately set aside time to spend with other people to build familiarity and closeness you can draw on when you need help. Also, you will have the chance to be a source of wisdom, support and sympathy when they need it, too. And that always feels good.

Finally, do consider the option of seeking professional advice and support when appropriate. People often resist the idea of working with a therapist, counsellor or coach. That is again usually because they are afraid this will be a sign of weakness. Nothing could be further from the truth. It's a sign of the flexibility of resilience.

Change is the only constant

Planning for change can create an illusion. The illusion is that when the plan comes to fruition all change will be over and you can settle into a lifetime of undisturbed stability. The reality is life will never be like that. Change is constant. Philosophers say it is the only constant. The Buddhists say:

> If you want to know the truth of life and death, you must reflect continually on this: there is only one law in the universe that never changes – that all things change, and that all things are impermanent.
>
> (Sogyal Rinpoche, *The Tibetan Book of Living and Dying*, p 29)

Also:

> Through weathering changes we can learn how to develop a gentle but unshakeable composure.
>
> (Ibid)

It's time to stop reacting to change with surprise and fear. Meet the challenge of constant change head on. When one plan is done, reach for the next. Welcome change as the only way that new and exciting experiences will arise and seek out the potential opportunities with 'gentle but unshakeable composure'.

KEY 4   SUMMARY

Change is the only constant

- Our evolutionary ancestors had a fight-or-flight reaction to change because change could indicate a real threat to their survival. People still react to change in the same way, even though most change is no longer life-threatening.

- The instinctive reaction to change is the D-type response that perceives change as DANGER.

- It is possible to overcome the D-type response and replace it with the O-type reaction where change is perceived as OPPORTUNITY.

- Change is a constant and inevitable characteristic of modern life. Cultivate O-type qualities to keep stress at bay. Do this by:

  1   looking for the good news in all change;

  2   making plans to deal with major change in life.

No man ever steps in the same river twice, for it is not the same river and he is not the same man.

HERACLITUS of EPHESUS

KEY 5

10

Life is difficult... And that's ok

People fear and avoid difficulty in life because they believe that they will be unable to cope. You need to know that you have the ability to deal with life's challenges with courage and confidence.

Our discussion of KEY 4 focused on the inevitability of change. Change is going to happen. In fact, it is happening right now. Something is changing somewhere in your life even as you read this sentence.

Sometimes changes are pleasant, whether they are anticipated or not, and obviously you don't need our help to enjoy those! But, often those changes are difficult. Change can bring unexpected challenges even when you know it is going to happen, and perhaps even initiated it yourself. Frequently though, the things that happen to you are unexpected and not what you would have chosen. Those events especially can bring about great disruption or loss.

CASE STUDY

Once my husband and I came back from a lovely relaxing holiday to discover that we had dry rot in our house. We realized that the rot had been spreading under the floors and up the walls for some time, causing widespread damage. We were extremely shocked and upset. The treatment for the rot involved a huge amount of destruction and rebuilding, and the upheaval and sense of loss were immense as we saw our home turned suddenly into a building site.

I realized that, for a long time, while I presented this course and told people that 'change is happening all the time', it really had been... in my own home... and I had no idea.

In the last chapter we explained that the only really effective way to handle change is to respond positively and flexibly. As you work to develop that resilient O-type approach, we hope you will find it helpful to use our KEY 4 advice on how to seek the good news and proactively make plans to face the challenges of change.

There was something else we encouraged you to do when faced with change. Can you remember what that was? Write it down here if you can:

....

....

....

....

We explained that change is a powerful trigger for stress because it threatens people's need for control. That's because the 'need to know' is an important aspect of people's need for control, and there is so often a great element of the unknown when things change. When D-type people are faced with the unknown they try to regain a sense of control by filling in the gaps in their knowledge. They imagine what is happening or what is going to happen. The problem with this is, because they tend only to see the danger in change, they usually imagine the worst possible disasters. Then they believe themselves. It's as if what they imagine is reality. This triggers a perception that they won't be able to cope. Then they believe this, too. This whole process sets off their 'Can't cope!' fight-or-flight response, and allows it to continue to repeat over and over again. Since change is such a constant feature of life this can become a source of damaging chronic stress.

On the other hand, O-type people are able to focus on what they actually know about a situation and then do what they can to take control of that by looking for the potential opportunities and making plans. For the rest, they have the ability to let go of their need for control. They accept not knowing. They believe that, when they do know, they'll deal with it. In this way they replace the 'Can't cope!' perception with a strong sense that they *can cope*. This is the complete opposite of the perception that gives rise to stress. So the fight-or-flight response to change is interrupted and the build up of stress is avoided. Resilience is maintained and even allowed to grow and develop.

Now, this is another point in our face-to-face courses when people challenge us with, 'Yes but, that's easier said than done.' And again we reply, 'Yes, it is.' If your perception of yourself is that you can't cope then it can be hard to go against your instinct and start to believe the opposite. But it can be done.

It's really a question of building your self-confidence so that when you tell yourself you can cope, you'll believe it.

Building self-confidence

If you're a person who finds it difficult to believe you can cope, let's see if we can convince you that you can. Here's a bold statement for you.

> Even though we've never met you, we know you have the ability to cope with everything life can throw at you.

How do we know?

> Because, you already have.

Not convinced?

That's ok. Actually we know that for us to say you can cope will not convince you if you truly fear that you can't. Self-confidence doesn't come from someone else telling you that you can do something. It comes from self-awareness. This is the knowledge that comes from within you yourself of your qualities, skills, experience and expertise in life. So we need to find another strategy to help you to believe in your ability to cope.

There are two reasons why people might doubt their ability to cope.

1. Coping versus keeping calm

When people have developed a strong belief that they are unable to cope with the challenges of life it is often because they confuse 'coping' with 'keeping calm', or with 'finding it easy'.

This means, for example, that if they became distressed or angry during a difficult time, and were perhaps emotional and wept or shouted, they interpret this as having 'not coped' or 'coped badly' because they 'found it difficult' and didn't stay 'calm'. But, is 'coping' the same as keeping calm, or finding it easy? It is for a person who wishes to be strong, not for a person who prizes resilience.

Think back to Part One and our definition of resilience. There we said that resilience is:

> ... not the same as strength, which enables you to remain calm, unaffected, or 'stony' in the face of life's difficulties and challenges. Rather it is that you are moved emotionally by those difficulties – you feel pain, anxiety, fear, sadness, even despair – and then can *recover to your original state*.

We also said:

> At its best resilience enables a person to recover to an *even more resourceful state*. This happens when the person can use a difficult experience to become more aware of their personal qualities, skills and abilities, and able to use those more readily and fully when they are challenged again in the future.

So when we say we know you have the ability to cope with everything life can throw at you, we don't mean we believe you have the ability to remain calm no matter what happens. We mean we know you can come through even though you will find life very emotionally tough at times. We mean even though you may be sad, angry, frustrated, irritated, anxious, desperate, or a mixture of many different emotions, you can recover. More than that, you can use those experiences to become more aware of, and build on, your personal qualities and skills.

2. *Coping versus managing alone*

Another very common reason for people's belief that they are unable to cope with life's challenges is that they confuse 'coping' with 'managing alone'. So if they ever had to get help to overcome a difficulty they think this means they 'couldn't cope'.

As we've said before, sometimes an event or situation can be so overwhelming that it is actually more than you can handle. However, this is not a reason to allow your fight-or-flight mechanism to keep on repeating and raising your stress levels with fear. You don't have to manage everything on your own. It is a sign of flexibility and resilience to recognize when you are truly out of your depth and to ask for help, support or even just a compromise from someone else.

Family, friends and colleagues are there for you as you are there for them. There is also a huge range of qualified, professional people out there who have all the knowledge and skills required to help you out.

> People I worked with in my psychotherapy practice would very often say that the fact they'd had to come into hospital or to my clinic to see me was a clear sign they couldn't cope with life. I used to reply, 'This is how you are coping, by coming here for help!'

When we say we know you have the ability to cope with everything life can throw at you, we don't mean we believe you have the ability to be able to deal with everything on your own. We mean that you can cope with everything precisely because you are not alone.

Are you closer now to being convinced of your ability to cope with everything life throws at you? Can you see that you already have?

If you're still not sure, the next exercise will give you all the clear evidence you need.

Exercise thirteen

In a moment we're going to ask you to think about a time in your life when you experienced something difficult. It doesn't have to be the most awful experience you've ever had, and please don't go into your darkest memories. This exercise will apply to those very traumatic experiences too, but you don't need to start there. Take care of yourself and think of a time that feels easier to work with. If you find yourself thinking about something that is too painful to recall then take a break. Go and do something else for a while. When you come back you can start with a different memory.

It's important that this event happened in the past and it's over. It was hard at the time. Perhaps life threw something at you out of the blue; something like an accident, or a flood, or a burglary, etc. Maybe someone close to you decided to make a change in their life that affected you in ways that were very challenging or hurtful. On the other hand, perhaps you made a decision yourself to instigate a change in your life; to change a relationship, or where you lived, or your job, etc. Maybe that was a difficult time because of other people's reactions or because you had to suffer some loss in order to gain what you wanted.

CASE STUDY

One day I was giving a talk to a group of university lecturers and I noticed one of them talking on their mobile phone. During the coffee break this delegate came up to me and apologized. She said it must have seemed very rude, but as I was talking she realized that she had identified her young daughter as the most important and precious thing in her life and yet she hardly saw her child because she was away so often at conferences. She'd felt she had to call her husband right away to cancel childcare as she had decided not to go to yet another conference the next week.

So this delegate had herself instigated a change. She did that because she believed it would reduce her stress, and make life easier and more pleasant for herself and her family. But it would also bring some challenging consequences.

Can you imagine the kinds of challenges the person would face to make this decision in a competitive university environment? In terms of approval? How about in terms of control? What could she potentially lose in making that decision?

I discovered some months later that she had left her very high-status, well-paid academic post so that she could be at home even more with her family and fulfil her own personal goal of further study. What kinds of challenges and loss might she have faced in taking this step?

Perhaps things became so difficult that you believed you wouldn't be able to cope. You believed you'd never get through such an experience and you'd never recover.

Yet you did cope. You did get through it, and you have recovered. You resolved the difficulty, or you moved on in spite of the fact that it couldn't be resolved.

This is not to say that the experience has been without consequences and perhaps even lasting effects on you personally. Just as physical injuries leave scars on the body, so life events can leave psychological and emotional scars. Remember though that this is not about finding life easy. It's about finding it very difficult sometimes, and recovering from that. You may be scarred, but you are here.

It may even be that you are able to notice ways in which you have benefited from having gone through that experience. Perhaps you gained new relationships or opportunities to do things that you hadn't imagined at the time. Or maybe you recognize some personal strengths or abilities that you have now as a direct result of what you went through then.

So, with all those prompts in mind, think about a time in your life when you experienced something difficult. Then answer the questions in boxes 1 and 2 below. When we present this exercise to live groups we ask people to work in pairs because sometimes it can help to talk through the questions initially. This enables them to clarify what happened and what the feelings were at the time. Also, we know that people can be reluctant to identify really positive things about themselves and it can help to have someone else there to point out their skills and qualities. So it might be easier for you too to go through the exercise with a trusted friend or colleague. If you find it a useful process for yourself then perhaps you could do the same for them to help to give their confidence a boost too.

NB It is very important that you are able to complete both boxes in one period of time without taking a break in between. So only start with the questions in Box 1 now if you are not in a rush and will be able to finish Box 2 as well. Otherwise, leave it and come back when you do have time.

Dealing with a difficult time: how did you do that?

Box 1

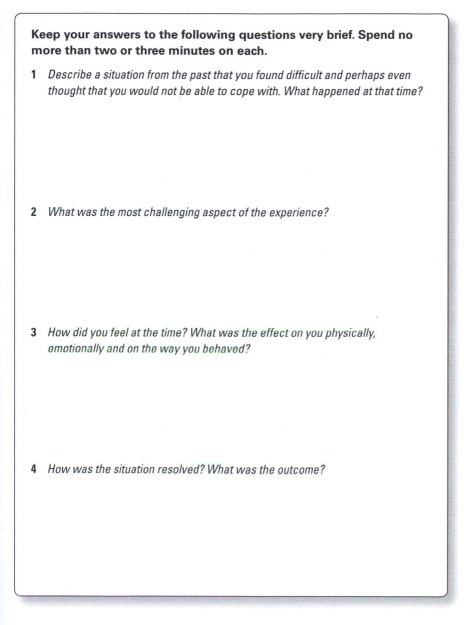

Keep your answers to the following questions very brief. Spend no more than two or three minutes on each.

1   *Describe a situation from the past that you found difficult and perhaps even thought that you would not be able to cope with. What happened at that time?*

2   *What was the most challenging aspect of the experience?*

3   *How did you feel at the time? What was the effect on you physically, emotionally and on the way you behaved?*

4   *How was the situation resolved? What was the outcome?*

Now go straight on to Box 2.

Box 2

> **Provide more detailed answers to the next questions. Take time to consider, remember and perhaps ask others. Write down everything you can in response.**
>
> 1   *What role did you play in managing that situation? What did you do?*
>
> 2   *What personal skills, qualities, knowledge and experience did you use to enable you to deal with that difficult situation?*
>
> 3   *If you had support from others, who helped you (professional and/or personal support)?*
>
> 4   *In what ways can you see you have benefited from having gone through that experience – in relationships, opportunities, personal strengths or abilities?*

Well done! We'd like you to fill in just one more box and then we'll reflect on the exercise as a whole. You can take a break before this one if you like.

When you are ready, look again at your answers to these particular questions from Box 2:

What personal skills, qualities, knowledge and experience did you use to enable you to deal with that difficult situation?

and...

If you had support from others, who helped you (professional and/or personal support)?

Write down everything you wrote in answer to those questions again in Box 3 below. If you can think of any more things to add while you are doing this then write them down in the box too. Write in big bold letters. You might even grab a handful of coloured markers and use different colours and styles so your box is fun to fill in and eye-catching.

If you are like most of the people who do this exercise with us on our courses then your box might look something like this... (only perhaps in bright, bold colours)....

courage   looking forward   **self-belief**   talking to others   determination
honesty   family   **managing time**   sense of humour   **planning**
having a goal   understanding   **perspective**   awareness   compassion
ability to get things done   got angry   energy   professional advice
friends   self time   having fun   helping others   *stubbornness*
having a good cry   **knowing it would end**   love

Fill yours in on the next page now.

Box 3

Reflect

Now take some time to think about that exercise and reflect for a few minutes each on the following questions:

Q1. When was the last time you thought about this particular difficult experience in the way that you did in Box 2; that is, in terms of your ability to come through it and the support you had along the way?

Q2. What does it feel like to have thought about the experience in that way now?

Q3. If you had to face another difficult situation in the future, or indeed if you are facing one now, what skills, qualities, knowledge and experience will you use to get through it?

Q4. Given all that you have written in Box 2 and reinforced in Box 3, what is there that could happen in your life that you genuinely would not be able to cope with (ie that you would not be able to survive)?

Now let's explore these questions a bit further.

Q1. When was the last time you thought about this particular difficult experience in the way that you did in Box 2; that is, in terms of your ability to come through it and the support you had along the way?

It is very rare that someone can honestly say they've spent time thinking about past experiences in terms of their personal skills and qualities, the support they've had from others and the benefits they've gained as a result of that experience.

Much more frequently people say one of two things. Either they haven't thought about their example at all for a long time or, if they have thought about it, they have tended to ruminate only on the negative aspects of the event and of what they did and how they felt. They've thought over and over again about how awful it was and about what they wish they'd done differently. They've felt the painful emotions of that time over and over again.

This repeated focus on such negative elements of past experiences powerfully undermines a person's confidence in their ability to deal with difficulty in life. This in turn enhances their perception that they are unable to cope. This means that whenever they are faced with difficulty in life they become fearful and stressed.

In their everyday lives people rarely decide consciously and deliberately to think about difficult experiences from their past. They tend to try to avoid those memories because it is usually painful and upsetting to re-live those times. This exercise is a way of re-living those times that leaves you feeling positive about yourself, and confident and energized to deal with whatever is happening in the present or might happen in the future.

You don't need to wait to be asked to think about it as we've just done. Every now and again, in a quiet moment, deliberately remind yourself of a difficult time and of all the great skills and qualities you used to survive it. When faced with a challenging situation, use your long route thinking brain to interrupt your immediate fear response. Acknowledge the painful emotions involved and then right away focus on how you can and will survive. Why will you believe that? You'll believe it because, many times and in many different ways, you already have.

Q2. *What does it feel like to have thought about the experience in that way now?*

We hope it felt good for you to think about your past experience in a positive way, and that you felt encouraged and even proud of yourself. Perhaps you were surprised to be able to identify resources that you've never been aware of before. People spend more than enough time beating themselves up about not being good enough. It's wonderful for your self-esteem and self-confidence if you've discovered that you are, in fact, more than good enough in ways that you never even realized.

CASE STUDY

Going back to my story of the dry rot experience, I must say I found the shock and upheaval very difficult at the time. When the surveyor was about to tell us what he had found he said, 'there'll be tears...', and there were. My instinctive response was to feel threatened and as though I wouldn't be able to cope because there was so much that was out of my control.

However, during the months of house treatment and repair, I discovered great resources within myself that I didn't realize I had. I found I had the ability to plan and organize and co-ordinate a complicated process that involved a number of different people over several months. I had to look ahead and communicate clearly. I needed to manage my own time effectively so I could oversee developments while I carried on working. I discovered levels of determination, focus and energy that surprised me. I never knew I could be so good at project management. I realized I'm a person who can get things done!

Some months after this experience I was involved in a car accident. My car was damaged when two other cars collided close by. In the past I would have been upset and stressed by the process of getting through all the inconvenience and hassle of insurance and repairs, etc. Other people were concerned, but I just thought, 'It's only another project, and I'm more than good enough to deal with it.'

Q3. If you had to face another difficult situation in the future, or indeed if you are facing one now, what skills, qualities, knowledge and experience will you use to get through it?

We hope your answer to this question would be, 'I will use the same personal skills, qualities, knowledge and experience that I used in the past.'

Actually, you have more of all those resources now than you had then. The experience you thought of for this exercise, and others that have followed it, have enhanced your skills and qualities. The truth is that you are better equipped now to deal with a difficult life event than you have ever been before. You have the ability to cope with everything life can throw at you. Do you believe that now?

CASE STUDY

A woman who attended one of our confidence-building courses many years ago said the reason she attended the course was so that she could be confident that her husband would be faithful to her. She had been betrayed before and was afraid it would happen again.

I told her there was no training course in the world that could give her that kind of confidence. I told her she could hope he would be faithful and that she could count on him to live by the promises they had made to each other. But no one knows what will happen in the future. She could never know that he would be faithful, or for that matter that she would be faithful to him (if it had been her husband who had come to me I would have said the same to him).

All she could know, and all she really needed to know, was that whatever happened she would be able to handle it. It would be devastating... and she would cope. How? With all the skills, qualities, knowledge and support she used when it happened in the past, plus all of those she has developed since then.

With that kind of self-confidence she could get on with living her life and loving her husband without the constant emotional drain of the fear of being unable to cope with something that is so out of her control.

And finally:

Q4. *Given all that you have written in Box 2 and reinforced in Box 3, what is there that could happen in your life that you genuinely would not be able to cope with (ie that you would not be able to survive)?*

After all that reflection we hope your response to this question is something like, 'Not very much.' That's what people in our groups most often say at this point. Sometimes they even say, 'Nothing at all!'

There really is very little indeed that could happen to you that you would not be able to cope with, either on your own, or with help from others. There is a lot that could happen that might cause you to become angry, even furious; or sad, even desperately so. It is human and healthy to feel these emotions if you engage with all that makes life the rich, fulfilling and joyful experience you want it to be. You must feel sadness if you have joy. You must experience loss if you feel love, frustration if you have a passion, anger if you have a sense of justice. In other words, to feel all the 'good' you have to accept the 'bad'. That's life. It's time to stop expecting life to be easy and then reacting with surprise and fear when it turns out to be tough sometimes.

Life is difficult, and that's ok. It's ok because you don't need to be afraid. Fear comes from your perception that you will be unable to cope, and that comes from your sense of being out of control. But even when it appears that there is nothing you can control, there is in fact one thing that you can always control. You can always control the perception you have about how well you are able to cope. You need never believe that you can't cope because now you know you can. Even in a life that is complex and ever-changing, that's all you need to know.

We hope that, as you have worked through the preceding four KEYS, you have taken the time to pause and reflect on how the ideas behind each of the KEYS apply to you and to your life.

Perhaps you have been able to identify with the suggestion that people are powerfully driven by their needs for approval and control. You might have been able to recognize which of the two needs is your most influential driver, and have become aware of the effect that has had on your levels of stress and ability to maintain resilience.

You may have discovered, as do many people who attend our courses, that you are putting too much of your time and energy into aspects of your life that are simply not very important to you personally and that, as a result, life is slipping by while you postpone the really meaningful activities or relationships in your life. Maybe you have always had a dream or desire to do something extraordinary and different, but have not taken steps to make that dream a reality for you. You might have realized that there is an area of your life (perhaps your job, a close relationship, your wider family, your home or environment) that has become very unhappy or even damaging, and yet you say nothing.

Using what you've learnt from KEY 5, can you see now that you can take whatever steps you need to take, however difficult, to create a life for yourself that is more fulfilling and less stressful both for yourself and those close to you?

Can you see that you have all the resources you need to deal with change and even to introduce it into your life? Can you recognize that you have all you need to be able to state your intentions clearly with empathy and without apology, to say 'no', or to challenge an abusive or bullying relationship, with the self-confidence to know that you can deal with any consequences that might arise as a result?

On the other hand, can you see that you have all the skills, qualities and experience you need to be able to tell someone else how wonderful they are, and even that you love them? To communicate to people when you want or need support, understanding or help, no matter how they might react?

We warned you at the beginning of this book that the KEYS would be challenging and we expect you've found that to be the case. We've encouraged you to let go of needs and fears that are profoundly instinctive and powerfully habitual. We've invited you to go against those instincts so you can take control of your life and stand up for your own rights and values while allowing others the same freedom. We've asked you to welcome change and even to instigate it where you see areas of unhappiness or dissatisfaction in your life and relationships. With KEY 5 we hope we've helped you to build your confidence in your ability to do those things.

When something happens to you, or when you take action to make something happen, you can never know for certain what the outcome will be. It might be easier or even tougher than you can imagine. Now you know that it will be ok either way. If it turns out to be easier that's ok. You can relax and enjoy the relief. If not, that's also ok. You'll deal with it.

KEY 5   SUMMARY

Life is difficult... And that's ok

- People are afraid of difficulty in life because they have a sense that they won't be able to cope. They confuse 'coping' with keeping calm, or managing everything without help from others.

- Everyone has coped with challenges in life. Use your past experiences to build your self-confidence so you can believe that you will cope with whatever life throws at you.

- To build self-confidence remind yourself of all the great skills and qualities you used to survive a difficult time. Re-live those times in a way that leaves you feeling positive about yourself and confident that you will deal with whatever happens in the future.

- Don't expect life to be easy, and then react with surprise and fear when it turns out to be difficult. Instead, expect it to be difficult and trust in your abilities to deal with it – it's just life.

Once we truly know that life is difficult, once we truly understand and accept it, then life is no longer difficult.

M SCOTT PECK

KEY 6

11

Attitude makes all the difference

You often can't change your circumstances, but you always have a choice about your attitude. If you change the way you think, you will change the way you feel. That makes all the difference.

We talked a lot about perception as we presented the last two KEYS. In KEY 4 we compared D-type people, who perceive only danger when they are faced with change, with O-type people who perceive change as opportunity. In KEY 5 we explained how the perception of danger in a situation leads to a further perception of being unable to cope, not only with change, but also with any difficulty that arises in life. This is the perception that gives rise to stress. So people who are prone to feel that they can't cope are very vulnerable to chronic stress.

On the other hand, a perception that change brings opportunity, along with the ability to let go of the need to be in control of everything and to just deal with things as they arise, leads to a strong sense of being able to cope. People who are able to perceive changes and difficulties in their lives in these ways reduce their stress and let resilience flourish instead.

So, our aim in KEYS 4 and 5 was to enable you to become aware of your own perceptions of danger and of being unable to cope, and to confront and change them. We couldn't tell you to stop those perceptions arising because they are instinctive reactions that happen at an unconscious level. Instead we encouraged you to engage your brain's long route and give yourself time to think when you become aware of feelings of fear or of becoming overwhelmed. In KEY 4 we gave you a number of strategies to help you learn to be an O-type and in KEY 5 we took you through a process that, we hope, showed you that you have all the resources you need to cope with anything life can throw at you. As you read our suggestions and worked on the exercises you were using your thinking brain to discover more appropriate responses to events and situations that you would otherwise react to with fear. In a nutshell, you were using your thinking brain to *choose your attitude*.

In this chapter we'll explore what it means to be able to choose your attitude and we'll look at some different techniques you can use to do that. We'll begin by talking about what we mean by the word 'attitude' and why it is such an important concept in the development of resilience.

Attitude

1. What is attitude?

As usual, we'd like to give you a chance to think about your own definition before we reveal ours.

Write down here what you think the word 'attitude' means:

....

....

....

....

We'll be looking at two different aspects of the idea of 'attitude'.

We expect you'll have written down something about a person's thoughts about things; their interpretation of events or the way they view themselves or other people. We'd agree. It is a person's state of mind with regard to an event, person or object. It's what they think or believe about something.

But, you may have mentioned another aspect of 'attitude' that people we speak to are less likely to identify. A person's attitude is also their physical posture, facial expression and the way they communicate. It's their behaviour; the way they express how they are feeling or reacting to something or someone.

These two features of 'attitude' are closely linked and we'll explain how later. For now we'll look at the power of attitude and why, as the KEY says, it 'makes all the difference'.

2. The importance of attitude in developing resilience

Attitude is important in building resilience because *the way you think affects the way you feel*. Even more crucial is the fact that you have the ability to choose your attitude. That means you have the power to control the way you feel.

This is a reality that has been recognized for many centuries. In fact, the idea was written down as far back as the 2nd century AD in a book called *Meditations* by the Roman Emperor, Marcus Aurelius. In this book of reflections on philosophy and what is now termed psychology, Aurelius says:

> If you suffer distress because of some external cause, it is not the thing itself that troubles you but your judgement on it...

He's saying that the way you think about something affects how you feel more than the thing itself. But then, again more crucially, he says:

> ... and it is within your power to cancel that judgement at any moment.

It is within your power to cancel that judgement at any moment. To lessen your distress you can decide, at any time, to think about something in a different way.

The theory that it is a person's thoughts and beliefs about things rather than the things themselves that cause feelings of fear, anxiety or distress, and that you can choose to stop or change those thoughts and beliefs, was introduced to modern psychology in the 1960s in the form of Cognitive Therapy. So we were amazed to discover that it was recognized by someone two-thousand years ago – and he probably wasn't the first. We're telling you about this because it shows that:

1 people have been struggling with the psychological causes of stress for thousands of years;

and

2 to recognize the influence of attitude on emotions, and to take control of that, is one solution to stress and distress that has really stood the test of time.

Cognitive Therapy is currently used as a form of psychotherapy treatment for severe stress, anxiety and depression. The therapy focuses on a person's thoughts and beliefs about themselves, their lives, their relationships, etc. (It is called 'Cognitive' because, in psychology, thoughts and beliefs are called 'cognitions'.)

If we add the element of 'attitude' that is about behaviour as well as thoughts, you may be able to recognize the most widely recognized modern-day form of this approach as Cognitive-Behavioural Therapy (CBT). Don't worry if you are not familiar with this. We will now explore what it is and how it works in some detail.

CBT: changing thoughts to change feelings

In KEYS 4 and 5 you have already been through a process to help you to become aware of perceptions that you have which create fear and stress, and to learn strategies to help you to change those perceptions. In essence what we were saying in those KEYS was that it isn't change or a difficult situation that causes you to be stressed; it's your perception of it or your ability to cope with it (or, as Marcus Aurelius would say, 'your judgement on it'). Then, when we presented our plan for change in KEY 4 and our exercise in KEY 5 to recall how you dealt with a past difficulty, we were really saying that you can take control of those perceptions and change them so you feel more optimistic and confident in yourself ('it is within your power to cancel that judgement...'). This is exactly what CBT does. It encourages people to recognize thought patterns, perceptions or interpretations that lead them to feel unnecessarily stressed, distressed and even depressed, and then to change those thoughts and interpretations so they feel better and more self-confident.

The important word in the above paragraph is 'unnecessarily'. It is not the aim of CBT (nor of KEY 6) to tell you to take a mindlessly positive attitude to everything you do, and to get you to feel calm, or good and happy about everything that happens to you. CBT acknowledges that it is sometimes appropriate to feel upset, angry or even desperate at times. You need to feel those emotions when dreadful things happen. You need to recognize when your perception that you can't cope is right and you are truly overwhelmed and need support.

CASE STUDY

I was asked to provide CBT psychotherapy for a young man who had been involved in a terrible car accident. His best friend was driving the car when they were hit head-on by another vehicle at some speed. The young man was very severely injured and he spent the best part of three months in a coma following the crash. When he emerged from the coma he discovered that his friend had been killed in the accident. He was understandably devastated by this tragedy. When he eventually went home he withdrew from family and friends and spent most of his time shut away in his room. After a few months his parents became concerned about his behaviour and sought CBT because they had heard it could achieve quick results.

The first time I saw this young man it was clear that it was too soon. He needed to spend a great deal more than a few months grieving, with all the despair, rage and bitterness that involved for him. He didn't want to be 'treated' or 'fixed' and I couldn't blame him. I recommended a different kind of more long-term support for him and his family.

CBT steps in to help change those feelings only when they are the result of perceptions, thoughts and interpretations that, in some way, do not reflect the reality of a situation (eg the D-type 'It's all terrible!', when it isn't) or the qualities and abilities of the person involved (eg 'I don't have the personal resources to deal with difficulty', when they do). In CBT these are called 'irrational thoughts' because they don't fit with what is happening in the real world. They don't make sense in relation to the reality of a situation or the nature of the person involved. When this is the case, CBT tries to guide people to adopt a more rational or realistic attitude. So, the shift of attitude is not from negative to positive. It is from unrealistic to realistic.

We are going to present some examples to illustrate so that you can understand this very clearly.

CBT and the three Ps

The examples we would like to give you of the way CBT works will lead us to a topic we haven't looked at yet in this book; that is, depression. We are introducing it now because depression is very closely related to stress. In fact, depression is the mental illness that is most commonly experienced by people who suffer from severe or chronic stress.

When we talked about the relationship between stress and resilience in our Introduction we described it as a 'vicious cycle' where lack of resilience leads to stress, which lowers resilience further, which makes it more likely that a person will respond to difficulty by becoming stressed, which lowers resilience even further, etc.

For some people, stress undermines their resilience so much that they are totally depleted. They have no resources left to bring to the challenges of life, and this leads them to feel helpless and hopeless. Feelings of helplessness and hopelessness are the classic signs of depression.

It might be helpful to look at the relationship between stress and depression as another kind of vicious cycle. Stress is the result of instinctive fear that is reinforced by people's unrealistic negative thoughts about their lives (eg 'It's all terrible!') and about themselves (eg 'I can't cope, I'm useless!'). When people continue to think in these ways they begin to feel helpless and hopeless. When people feel helpless and hopeless they are more likely to respond to challenges with fear and unrealistic negative thoughts, which increases their sense of being helpless and hopeless... and so on.

We are going to look more closely now at some of the unrealistic thoughts that people begin to develop when they are stressed and which are reinforced in depression. We'll also show you the way that CBT counters these thoughts with more realistic interpretations.

We'd like you to explore these with us in the form of a reflective exercise.

Exercise fourteen

When CBT was first developed in the 1960s, the psychologists who created the model found that the unrealistic thoughts revealed by people who were vulnerable to stress and depression could be grouped into three categories, which are called 'thinking styles' or 'thinking patterns'. These thinking styles have been given different names by therapists since then, but it might be easiest for you to remember them as the 'Three Ps'. The Three Ps are **Permanent**, **Pervasive** and **Personal**. In contrast to each of these thinking styles, CBT offers three more realistic approaches; **Flexible**, **Specific** and **External**.

We will describe the three unrealistic thinking styles and the alternative interpretations suggested by CBT. From time to time we'll ask you to make some notes on your personal reflections as you read.

From our explanations you might discover that you have a tendency to think along the lines of one or more of the Three Ps and would like to change that, but don't know how. Put that aside for the moment and just read and note your reactions and reflections as you go. We promise to present some strategies and techniques to enable you to adopt a different and more helpful attitude later.

The Three Ps

1. Permanent vs Flexible

The permanent thinking style is shown when people believe that the way life is at the moment is the way it will always be. They think things will never change. The words 'always' and 'never' are classic indications that someone has a permanent thinking style. So people who have this thinking style believe that anything negative or unpleasant that's happening will continue forever. ('Forever' is another classic indication.) If they're ill they will always be ill. If they're unhappy they will always be unhappy. If they're alone they will always be alone. If things are difficult with a relationship or their finances, they will always be difficult.

Another characteristic of people who have a permanent thinking style is that they use past experiences to predict what will happen in the future. For example, if they've been unsuccessful in a test or exam then they believe they might as well give up because they will never succeed. If they've been unable to find a job or relationship in the past, they believe they might as well stop looking because they'll never find a job in the future. Have you ever thought you wouldn't get a parking space in town because you didn't get one last time? It's a more trivial example, but it demonstrates the same thing.

Do you recognize any of these kinds of permanent style of thoughts in your reflections on your own life? If so, write a brief description of an example or two. How do you feel when you think in these ways?

....

....

....

....

What's important to remember is that it isn't the illness, or the difficulty in finding a job or relationship that leads to depression. It is natural to feel unhappy, concerned or anxious if you are faced with any of these. The danger is if you start to believe that these circumstances will continue in exactly the same way forever. This leads to the feelings of helplessness and hopelessness that increase stress and can result in depression.

In contrast, people who have a flexible thinking style recognize the truth of our KEY 4 – that change is the only constant. They believe that nothing in life stays the same forever because things are constantly changing. This is true of situations, emotions, and physical and mental states. They understand that it is not possible to predict the future from what has happened in the past. The future will not be the same as the past because something will have changed. Again, using that trivial parking example, they'd think 'well, I didn't get parked last week but the traffic won't be exactly the same now so I might get lucky this time.'

Do you have any of these kinds of flexible style of thoughts? If so, write a brief description of an example or two. How do you feel when you think in these ways?

If not, do you think the alternative interpretations offered by CBT are more realistic; more true to life? How do you imagine you would feel if you thought in these more realistic ways instead?

....

....

....

....

This flexible style allows people to be hopeful for the future, even in areas where they have been unable to succeed in the past. They simply have not succeeded... *yet.*

Of course, things don't always change for the better. Sometimes they get worse. Again, the aim of CBT and this KEY is not to get you to 'Think Positive'. The aim is to encourage you to develop an open and flexible thinking style that means you can be hopeful (the opposite of the depressive hopeless) while at the same time you recognize that you really don't know what will happen. All you know is that whatever happens, you have all the resources you need to deal with it (the opposite of the depressive 'helpless').

CASE STUDY

There was a time when I had to be admitted to hospital with a serious infection. I was in constant severe pain, and was treated for several days with very strong antibiotics and painkillers. However, as the days went on, nothing seemed to relieve the pain, which kept returning just as badly whenever the painkillers wore off. On about the fourth day I found myself thinking that I would be in exactly the same pain *forever*. I began to feel hopeless and helpless, and that brought me very low. Then I thought, 'Hold on a moment. You really don't need to add depression to the awfulness of this situation! Nothing ever is the same forever. Things always change. This pain will either get better or it will get worse. If it gets better, that will be wonderful. If it gets worse the doctors will find out why and do something about it. Of course that will be difficult, but you have all the personal resources and support you need, and you will deal with it.'

Nothing had changed except my attitude. I was still very ill and in pain. But there was a change in the way I felt. Although I continued to feel anxious and unhappy, the sense of hopelessness eased away. Instead I felt hopeful and trusted my resilience. I'm sure you can imagine how my mood lifted as a result. I felt lighter and stronger. Every time I slipped back into that permanent way of thinking, I cancelled it and adopted the more flexible style. That made all the difference.

2. Pervasive vs Specific

The pervasive style is one that you can recognize from an all-or-nothing way of thinking. People who demonstrate this thinking style have three key characteristics.

1. They find it hard to see individual differences. So if one person betrays them they can't trust anyone. If a friend hasn't been in touch for a while then no one cares. If one employer has been difficult to work with, all employers are difficult.

How often do you think in these ways? How do you feel when you do that?

....

....

....

....

When a person is unable to perceive individual differences they can develop a strong sense of hopelessness as they begin to lose their ability to feel safe in any situation, or worthy of anybody's affection. As you know, this degree of loss of control and of other people's affection would be a profound cause of stress.

On the other hand, the more realistic perceptions that CBT offers take into account the potentially different qualities of specific people and situations. People who have a more specific thinking style believe that each situation and person will be different, and that it is unrealistic to expect a whole group of people to behave in exactly the same way as the one person who let them down. Again, this is not a 'Pollyanna', positive thinking approach. People who have a specific style don't just mindlessly assume that every person or situation they encounter will be wonderful. They just expect each situation and person to be different.

Can you imagine how this more specific style of thinking would lead someone to remain hopeful, while trusting their own ability to cope if they are let down? Make a note here of how you think that would feel. Or, if you have adopted this way of thinking, describe a couple of examples and say what you've felt when you've taken that approach.

....

....

....

....

2. People who have a pervasive style often struggle to separate different aspects of their lives that exist independently from each other. This means that if they are unhappy in one aspect of their life then everything in life is bad. If they're having a hard time in their relationship with their partner they find it difficult to enjoy the company of their friends or their work. If they have financial problems they can't enjoy even things that cost nothing, like special family moments or a walk in the park on a lovely day.

How easy do you find it to appreciate aspects of your life that are ok when there is a difficulty in one particular area? What does it feel like when unhappiness in one part of life spills over into all other aspects?

....

....

....

....

When people constantly feel unhappy, fearful, or anxious, no matter where they are or what they are doing, then they become very vulnerable to the experience of feeling overwhelmed. They begin to feel out of control of their lives. This triggers the perception of being unable to cope, which is the essence of stress. Also, there is a real risk of depression when a person suffers from unrelieved low mood for an extended period of time. If you do recognize that you have a tendency towards this kind of pervasive thinking then we would encourage you strongly to work towards adopting a different approach.

People with a more specific way of thinking are able to keep the different elements that make up their lives separate in their minds. This means that when things go wrong or they experience loss in one area of their lives, they realize this doesn't have to affect everything else. They see that while one specific part of life may be difficult, other aspects of life can remain un-affected by the problem and still be pretty good. If they are worried about something they don't allow that to affect the other things they enjoy. They don't see why they should let financial worries stop them enjoying a good chat and laugh with a friend. They recognize that it doesn't help their financial situation if they withdraw and spend all their time churning the problem over in their minds. They may feel unhappy or concerned at times, but these are limited to the moments when they are focused on difficult issues that they have to deal with.

If you tend to allow one area of difficulty to overwhelm everything else in your life, can you imagine how much more in control and resourceful you would feel if you could take a break from difficulties from time to time to relax and enjoy yourself?

3. The final pervasive style leads people to allow one element of life to define them. That one element takes on all-encompassing proportions instead of being just one of the many aspects of their lives, even if a very important one. So, for example, they believe that without their job or without their partner they are nothing. In a similar way they might allow their happiness to centre around one aspect of life. The garden, or a pet, or their house becomes the only thing that makes them happy.

Do you identify with this tendency to invest all your worth or happiness in one aspect of your life? If so, how do you feel in relation to that one aspect of your life?

....

....

....

....

The danger with this style of thinking is that nothing in life can be 100 per cent guaranteed to remain as it is forever. Remember, everything changes. Loss in any aspect of life is possible at any time. In fact, it is inevitable. If you let anyone or anything become the only thing that makes you happy then you are almost certainly destined to come to a time when there is nothing at all that will make you happy. If you let one element in your life define you then the risk is very high that, at some time in your life, you will experience yourself as being nothing or being worth nothing.

If you have this kind of pervasive tendency you will probably be aware of an element of fear underlying the love you have for that person or thing, or the joy or sense of self-worth it gives you. That's because, at some level, you know you might lose that person or thing, and there's nothing you can do about it. Even if you are not consciously aware of that fear, we believe it is always there at an unconscious level. As you now know, this continual underlying sense of lack of control is very stressful.

People with a more specific style of thinking recognize that their lives are extremely complex. There are many things that give them pleasure and even joy. Ok, maybe some more so than others. But they don't see even the most important and precious things in their lives as 'the only thing'. They know that if they lose something or someone that they cherish then they will be sad; maybe even desperately sad sometimes. But they know that they will recover and survive because there will always be other things remaining that can give some pleasure. They know that it is natural to grieve for the loss of something or someone that's important in their life, but they also know that, whatever happens and whatever they lose, they themselves are never nothing. There will always be something or someone left that will help them to maintain their sense of personal identity and self-esteem.

The major risk of this third kind of pervasive thinking is that it can lead a person with a vulnerability to depression to feel that there is no point in being alive when they lose the one thing that means everything to them. When I worked with people suffering with depression I used to suggest the following image as a way of looking at things differently.

When people feel overwhelmed by a situation and don't know where to start to deal with it, they quite often say, 'I can't see the wood for the trees!' This means they've got bogged down in the complicated details of something and they need to pull back and gain a view of the wider picture. Sometimes it can definitely help to do this. But sometimes it's the complicated details that really matter and you'll lose sight of those when you step back and see only the big picture.

Pervasive thinking is like flying high above the ground. From there you 'can't see the trees for the wood'. That's because, from a distance, it can look like a wood is made up of just one type of tree. On the other hand, specific thinking is like moving right into the middle of the wood. From that position you will see that there are many different types of tree and each is important in its own way.

Your own life is as complex as that wood. You could visualize your life as being made up of many different types of tree. Each type of tree would represent a different aspect of your life. So trees of one type are your partner, others are your children, your work, friends, pets, hobbies and so on. One aspect of your life might be so important to you that there are many of this type of tree in your wood. Indeed, there might be so many of one kind of tree that, from a distance, it looks like all of the wood is made up of this kind of tree. But, when you get right in and close up you'll be able to see all of the different types of tree growing there.

You may lose all of one kind of tree and that would be very sad. It would be natural for you to grieve for the loss of those trees. Look carefully though and you'll see that others are still standing. They are still alive and can give you shelter, support and protection. They may also need you to look after and nurture them. These make your life worth living.

Take a few moments to make a note of some of the different people and things in your life that you love and treasure, or that bring you joy or contribute to your sense of your identity and self-worth. Include even some things that seem of little importance but that bring you moments of pleasure or satisfaction.

....

....

....

....

....

....

How do you feel having completed that list? Do you feel that the CBT approach is more realistic than the pervasive style?

Different people have different emotional reactions when they think about the possible loss of things that contribute to their happiness and sense of well-being. Those who have a pervasive style imagine only devastating sadness, complete emptiness and even a loss of sense of self. People who think in a more specific way have a more poignant mixture of feelings. They can be very aware of the sadness that loss would bring, but can also see how that which remains could comfort and sustain them. We're sure you can see which of these attitudes reflects and builds resilience.

3. Personal vs External

The personal style of thinking is one that leads people to believe it's their fault if anything bad happens to them, or even to other people. When something unpleasant or unwanted occurs, they think it is because of something they have done wrong, or a mistake they have made. Sometimes, they believe it's their fault even when they've done nothing at all. It's just enough for them to be there. They think that there is something about who they are which brings about bad luck or misfortune. If they join a queue and it turns out to be the slowest, they'll think it's because they joined it. If it rains on a day they've planned a picnic, it'll be because it's their picnic. If their favourite football team loses it's because they supported the team. These are fairly trivial examples, but this kind of attitude can extend to much more serious situations; to real heartbreaking tragedies that happen in their own lives, in other people's lives, or even in the world in general. People who have a personal style blame themselves for their own or other people's illness or pain for example. Sometimes they can even feel responsible for someone else's loss of life. They believe that these unfortunate circumstances happen because they themselves are being singled out for unhappiness, or even that they are being punished for something. They couldn't say what they are being punished for or by whom, but they still feel that's what they believe.

Do you have any of these kinds of personal style of thoughts? If so, write a brief description of an example or two. How do you feel when you think in these ways?

....

....

....

....

The personal thinking style can lead people to be prone to unrealistic levels of pessimism and to an overwhelming sense of both hopelessness and helplessness. They lose their awareness of their own ability to be a force for good in their lives and in the world. No matter what they do, things will always turn out badly; not because that's just how things happen sometimes, but because they are there. This attitude can lead people to simply give up. What's the point in hoping or planning for something good when it is all bound to end in disaster anyway? They can be very hard on themselves and even punish themselves for making bad things happen that they had no influence over at all. At its most serious, this thinking style leads people who are vulnerable to depression to believe that everyone's lives would be better if they were not around at all. We know that one of the symptoms of depression is suicidal feelings and thoughts. The internal thinking style often underlies those feelings and thoughts.

On the other hand, there are people who have a more external thinking style. These people understand that bad things happen in life that have nothing to do with their own existence in the world, or their personal desires or qualities. They know it couldn't really be possible that their team lost because they were supporting the team. There are external factors, such as the skill of the players, who's injured, who's having a bad patch and not playing so well, the condition of the pitch, whether they're at their home ground or away and so on. There are many possible external causes for things like a queue slowing down or the weather turning bad, and people with an external attitude know this. They are able to examine a situation, take responsibility where they are actually personally responsible and let go when they are not.

Do you think the external interpretations that would be suggested by CBT are more realistic; more true to life? If you tend towards internal perceptions, how do you imagine you would feel if you thought in these more realistic ways instead?

....

....

....

....

The external way of thinking isn't a belief that everything will always turn out well. That's 'positive thinking', not 'realistic thinking'. But external thinking does leave room for people to hope and to maintain their sense of self-worth by recognizing their ability to act on the world in positive ways. The difference between an attitude that gives scope for hope and realistic personal empowerment and an attitude that takes those away can be all the difference between depressive illness and mental well-being.

CASE STUDY

There is a story from Eastern philosophy about a woman who lived in the time of the Buddha. This woman had a child who died and she was grief-stricken. She went to the Buddha weeping and begging him to heal her of her affliction. The Buddha told her that he could help her. What she had to do was to go to each of the houses in the village and collect a mustard seed from every house that had not felt the grief of bereavement.

The woman set out to collect the mustard seeds happy to think that she would be cured. Of course she returned to the Buddha with no mustard seeds at all since each of the families that she visited had experienced death in the family. Through this she learnt that suffering is a part of life for everyone. She wasn't being singled out for pain. She wasn't alone.

When you are suffering or in difficulty (even just irritated in a slow queue) it is easy to think that you are the only one who is suffering, and therefore there must be something wrong with, or bad about you and you are therefore marked out for unhappiness and pain. To develop an external thinking style you need first to realize that everyone has hard times and experiences difficult emotions. Simply by being human, everyone is marked out for suffering. Equally, everyone is marked out for joy. This is true for you no more nor less than it is true for anyone else.

Reflect

We have spent many years working with people who suffer from severe and/ or chronic stress and depression and we've seen the devastating effects of those conditions, not only on the individuals themselves but also on their friends, family and work colleagues – in fact everyone around them. So we know how important it is for people to understand what gives rise to these forms of mental ill-health conditions and to have strategies that really work to overcome and prevent them. That's why we have included the importance of attitude as one of our 7 KEYS, and taken time to explore the Three Ps and the CBT-type alternatives with you in some depth and detail. The practice of CBT is widely recognized to be a very effective way to tackle stress and depression, and the feedback we receive from our individual clients and from groups on our courses has consistently backed this up. People have told us and shown us that there is a great deal of truth in the theory behind the approach. We've seen how these ideas and strategies really do work.

Look at it this way. At any one moment in time there are an enormous number of people affected by either stress or depression, or both. Having said that, there are also a great many people who are not affected by either of these conditions. If we recognize that everyone has to deal with difficult times in their lives and that when they do they may feel a range of emotions; angry, sad, frustrated, frightened and so on, then we have to ask this question: if everyone experiences difficult events in their lives and experiences difficult emotions, how is it that not everyone becomes stressed or depressed?

It can't be the events themselves that cause stress and depression, even if those events are pretty terrible. If that were the case then everyone would suffer from stress and depression. In addition to the events, there must be something within an individual person that contributes to their mental and emotional response to those events. People experience stress and/or depression because they bring something of themselves to the events in their lives. They bring their attitude, and it's their attitude that makes the difference.

We hope you have become more aware of the kinds of thinking styles you are most likely to engage in (ie your attitude) and the effect that those kinds of interpretations can have on how you feel and on whether or not you respond with stress and/or vulnerability to depression. It would be very rare to find someone who thinks along the lines of the Three Ps in all circumstances or who has more flexible, specific and external thoughts no matter what happens. It is most likely that you've been able to identify in yourself some of each of the six types. But, we wonder if you noticed a stronger tendency towards Three Ps thinking and can recognize how that tendency leads you to feel low and lacking in resilience. If so, then you need to pay particular attention to the next section. Here we will describe some more of the kinds of thoughts you might have that could drain your resilience and, most importantly, some techniques you can practise to develop a more resilience-enhancing attitude.

Choosing your attitude

So far in this chapter we've been exploring what people think, and we guess that you have become more conscious of the kinds of things you think about yourself and about events as they take place in your life. Awareness is a good start, but of course it isn't the whole story. What do you do with that awareness if you've recognized that your approach is unhelpful and perhaps even harmful to your mental well-being?

Well, this KEY says that *you always have a choice about your attitude.* That means you have the ability to choose what you think. If you've discovered that you think along the lines of the Three Ps more often than you would like, you have the ability to change your attitude. But, how do you do that?

Up till now we've only looked at *what* people think. To explain what you can do to change what you think, we need to look at *how* people think. When you understand the mechanism behind your thought patterns you will discover a wide range of techniques to enable you to take control of your thoughts and choose the most realistic and appropriate responses. You will be able to 'cancel' judgements that cause you unnecessary distress and choose others that enable you to feel more capable and in control. This will protect your resilience and mental well-being in the face of life's challenges, and perhaps even give you the courage you need to take your life in the different and exciting directions you've always wished.

So...

How do people think?

At this point we would like to introduce a very popular modern philosopher called Eckhart Tolle. Eckhart Tolle's work has had a strong influence on our own thoughts about the power of attitude (and you will meet him in the next chapter too). Our interest in his approach began with an interview with Tolle that we read some time ago. During this interview he revealed that his philosophical journey began when he was a much younger man and suffering from deep depression and anxiety. He said that the more he actively looked for the answer to 'the dilemma of life' the more unhappy he became. Then at one point a thought came into his head. The thought was, 'I can't live with myself any longer.'

He went on to say that 'There seemed to be two of me – the "I" and this "self" that "I" cannot live with. Am I one or am I two?'

Suddenly it struck him that it was as if there must be one Eckhart Tolle who was ok and wanted to get on with things, and another Eckhart Tolle who was struggling and depressed, and who was being so heavy and such a pain in the neck that the first Eckhart couldn't live with him anymore! He asked himself 'Who am I? Who is this self that I cannot live with?'

Tolle had a moment of inspiration when he realized that the thought he'd had, 'I can't live with myself anymore', was simply an impression that came from what he called his 'pseudo self'. He was, of course, just one person; one self. This pseudo self was not an actual concrete entity. It wasn't real. It was just a voice expressing thoughts.

Tolle believes that everyone has this pseudo self. In fact, people are likely to have more than one of these 'selves' chatting away in their minds. Quite often these 'selves' don't agree with each other and have a constant, and not always harmonious, discussion with each other. This is how people think. They talk to themselves. Sometimes they do this out loud, but most often it is a conversation that takes place inside their head. That's why the voice that speaks your thoughts is often called the 'inner voice'.

Can you recognize this in yourself? For example, have you ever felt sorry for yourself? If the answer is 'yes', as it is for most people, then consider how strange that is. Who exactly is feeling sorry for whom? You can only work this trick by behaving in your mind as though there were two of you – one who is having a difficult or painful time, and another who is ok and feels pity for the one who is struggling. There may even be a third 'you' who doesn't feel sorry for the one who is in pain but prefers to tell that one to pull itself together! Here's another example. Have you ever felt cross with yourself? Again, you need to behave psychologically as if there were more than one of you – one who has done something wrong or unsuccessfully, and another who has done nothing at all but is watching and judging the one who has been acting in the world and who has let them down. Here again there might be a third 'you' who feels sorry for the first and begins to stand up for that one and offer reasons or excuses for its disappointing behaviour.

In a similar way, have you ever given yourself an instruction to do (or not do) something? For example, 'Do not eat that whole bar of chocolate!' Well, who is instructing whom? One of you is tempted and wants to eat the whole bar while another, who is not eating any chocolate, stands back and tells you not to. Then if you do eat the entire bar, the one who told you not to will be cross or disappointed. Then how does the you who ate the chocolate feel? That's right, the you who ate the whole bar feels guilty.

The voice, or voices, in your head are powerful because they affect the way you feel about yourself and your life. It is as if the voices belong to real people who are wiser and stronger than you are, and have the right to criticize or instruct you (sometimes a voice can sound like it comes from another person who has, or has had, authority over you; mother, father, etc). You feel that if these voices speak (whether in your own or in a different voice) you have to listen and take notice of what they say. So those voices have the power to lead you to feel confident and content, or unsure, fearful and unhappy.

In his darkest moment Eckhart Tolle had the realization that there was only one real self and that any thoughts he had about himself were only the voice of a pseudo self. There wasn't another Tolle who couldn't live with him. There was just one Tolle who could simply live or not live. He wanted to live. He found that by silencing the voice that told him he couldn't live with himself he was able to become, he said, 'deeply at peace'.

Now, as well as believing that everyone has a pseudo-self that talks to them in the form of thoughts, Tolle is also convinced that everyone has the ability to silence the constant chatter in their heads. He encourages people to let go of their thoughts about things and just 'be' with things as they are, in a kind of open awareness, without comment or judgement. He would say that as soon as you think something like, 'That's a beautiful sunset', or identify a plant or an animal by its species, you take something away from your pure experience of that thing. As soon as you name an emotion you feel such as, 'I am unhappy', you bring about a whole collection of evaluations, questions and analysis about your feeling of unhappiness that simply add weight and worsen your experience. He would say you need to silence the inner voice, to let go of thoughts, and just 'be'.

That is quite an extreme challenge for people who are used to having thoughts every moment of the day about everything from the greatest to the smallest aspects of their lives. If you feel that you would like to work towards Tolle's goal then we would encourage you to read more of his work and there are titles in our bibliography that you could follow up.

We have a wider goal though, one that we feel everyone is able to achieve. That is to be able to take control of the inner voice.

Taking control of the inner voice – what does that mean?

When the inner voice speaks, people usually listen to it. They take it seriously and believe what it says. But, one of the most exciting and liberating realizations that we have had as we've studied and worked in this field of psychology is that:

> Just because there is a voice speaking in your head doesn't mean it is saying something worth listening to.

Ok, sometimes it is saying something worth listening to. If we consider why people have an inner voice at all, from an evolutionary perspective its purpose is almost certainly to keep you safe from danger. If you were about to provoke a sabre-toothed tiger minding her cubs or single-handedly attack an unfriendly neighbouring tribe, the inner voice would have acted as the voice of caution saying, 'Don't do that, it's too risky!' And, of course there are still times when it is a good idea to listen to your inner voice and pay attention to what it says. If you've had a few drinks and are planning to drive, it would be a good idea to listen to your inner voice when it says, 'You'd better not do that.' It's a good idea to listen to the inner voice that urges caution when you are looking down from a great height, or trying to cross a busy road, or in any situation that warrants extra care. This doesn't have to involve the possibility of physical harm. The inner voice can protect you from risks to relationships, jobs, finances, etc. Quite recently I wrote an e-mail to someone while I was very distressed and angry and my inner voice told me not to send it... yet. I felt calmer the next day and was very glad I had listened to that voice. I could have caused a great deal of difficulty and upset if I had sent it.

So, we're not saying your inner voice never says anything useful – and that's why it's not necessarily always a good idea to silence or ignore it. But it is sometimes.

Taking control of the inner voice means that you:

1 *listen* to what it says;

2 *evaluate* the truth and usefulness of what it tells you;

3 *decide* whether or not you agree with what it told you in the first place.

You might decide that your inner voice is reflecting something realistic and useful for you. If so, then you should pay attention to it and act accordingly. On the other hand, you might recognize that the voice is saying something unrealistic and unhelpful. In that case you can choose to silence it completely, and we will describe techniques to enable you to do that if it seems appropriate. Or, rather than silence it, you might find it more constructive to get it to say something else, something more realistic and helpful. When you do this, the voice no longer belongs to a 'pseudo-self', but to your one real self. It is your own voice that reflects your own thoughtfully considered opinions and beliefs, and this is the only one that really counts. This is what it means to choose your attitude.

Remember my earlier story about when I was in hospital and in severe pain for a long period of time? Remember how I found myself thinking that I would be in exactly the same pain forever, and how that thought began to lead me to feel hopelessness and helpless?

Well, the inner voice has a powerful effect on emotions and behaviour because people tend to believe what it says and take its messages seriously. For a short while I took my inner voice seriously and felt very low as a result. But then I took control. I evaluated what it was telling me and decided it was not being realistic. I know the reality is that nothing ever is the same forever; that things always change. That's what I truly believe.

I told myself instead, 'This pain will either get better or it will get worse. If it gets better, that will be wonderful. If it gets worse the doctors will find out why and do something about it. Of course that will be difficult, but you have all the personal resources and support you need, and you will deal with it.' That was the voice of my one real self. I took that seriously instead and felt more able to cope.

Taking control of the inner voice – how do you do that?

We'd like to introduce you to three ways in which you can take control of your inner voice and, by doing so, choose your attitude. You may find that these take some work and practice because, as we've explained, you are possibly more used to letting your inner voice take control of you! However, if you are prepared to put the time and effort into mastering some or all of these techniques you will be well on your way to overcoming unnecessary stress and building your resilience.

Controlling your inner voice – 1

Become a scientist in your life

Above we described three steps to taking control of the inner voice. These were

1 *listen* to what it says;
2 *evaluate* the truth and usefulness of what it tells you;
3 *decide* whether or not you agree with what it told you in the first place.

Rather than simply accept what your inner voice says, we would suggest you see yourself as a kind of scientist who needs some evidence before you'll just go ahead and believe something that someone tells you – even if that someone sounds a lot like yourself.

An example to illustrate

Here's an example to illustrate the three steps in action. Let's imagine you walk past someone whom you know and they don't smile at you and you feel upset. Stop for a moment to...

1 *listen* to what your inner voice is saying.
   Do you immediately think that you must have done something wrong? What kind of Three Ps thinking style is this? Yes, it's 'personal'. Now you need to...

2 *evaluate* the truth and usefulness of that interpretation.
   It could be that the person has blanked you because you have done something that has annoyed or disappointed them. On the other hand, there could be an external explanation. So, ask yourself, do they not have a life outside of you and their relationship with you? Could they have had a difficult night, perhaps been unwell or had an argument with someone? Who knows? At this point, you don't know. So you don't have sufficient evidence to blame yourself and feel guilty or unhappy.

What is the one way you can get the evidence you need? Top marks if you are thinking 'Ask them.' We'd agree with that. The only way you will find out for sure is to ask the person involved. Just ask them how they are and if everything is ok because you noticed they didn't seem too happy when you saw them earlier. Then, when you have all the evidence you need, you can...

3 *decide* whether or not to agree with what your voice told you. You may find after all that the person is angry because of something you did or didn't do. In that case you will take steps to explain, apologize or take the necessary action. Or, you may find that the person is bothered by something completely separate from you. In fact, they may have been so distracted by their own inner voice (probably talking to them along the lines of one or other of the three Ps) that they didn't even notice you. Once you've discovered the real cause of their behaviour, your feelings will change and you will be able to act appropriately. If the answer is about you personally, that might not be pleasant but at least you will know and be able to take control of the situation. If the answer is about them and their own life you will be able to let go of any negative feelings about yourself that your personal thinking has generated and begin to focus on their needs and how you can help them instead.

CASE STUDY

A long time ago I attended a seminar presented by Dr Michael Yapko who is a very well-known and respected Cognitive-Behavioural specialist. At this seminar, Dr Yapko said this:

People think things, and then make the mistake of believing themselves.

He went on to say, 'And, they do this when they have little or no evidence for what they believe. Sometimes, they go on believing things even if they have information that flatly contradicts what they think!'

We think this is a great way to sum up the way that people generate an attitude that doesn't fit a situation or help them to deal with reality in an appropriate way – whether that's with joy or sadness, confidence or fear. As we said in KEYS 4 and 5, you need to get comfortable with being able to say 'I don't know.' If it isn't clear what is happening or why something has happened, if you can't point to some really good, solid, objective and reasonable evidence for your explanation, don't settle for making something up and then believing it. You deserve better than that.

Keeping a personal 'Thinking Styles Journal'

As you go through the three steps we've described, it can be very useful to keep a note of the process – just as scientists keep a record of their experiments and findings as they work. If you write things down it will enhance your awareness and reinforce the emotional and behavioural changes that you experience.

This strategy is the most commonly recommended by CBT. People who are engaged in this kind of therapy usually keep a journal that they fill in when they have difficult feelings. They write down what they are feeling in that moment, what they are thinking, what kind of thinking style their thoughts reflect, what evidence they have, what they decide to believe in the light of evidence and how they feel at that point.

You can keep your record in any way that suits you. The CBT journal usually looks something like this (we've used our examples to illustrate).

A journal to record my thoughts and feelings

Situation	How Do I Feel, What Do I Do?	What Am I Thinking?	What Thinking Style Is This?	Evidence To Support The Thought	Evidence Against The Thought	Alternative, More Realistic & Helpful Thinking Style	How Do I Feel, What Do I Do?
Walked past Kathy in the corridor, smiled at her but she just blanked me.	Upset and suspicious. I'm at my desk and don't want to talk to anyone.	I must have done something wrong and she wants to keep me in the dark about it. She doesn't like me. Nobody around here likes me.	Personal Pervasive	None. I don't know why she didn't smile at me.	I can't think of anything I might have done to hurt or upset her. And both Peter and Jo were friendly to me this morning.	**External:** There are lots of possible reasons for Kathy's behaviour that have nothing to do with me. **Specific:** Just because Kathy seemed unfriendly doesn't mean that no one likes me!	Better, calmer, kinder to myself. I'll just go and ask her how she is. Maybe I can help. If she's upset with me at least I'll know and can do something about it. Feel more in control.
In hospital. Been here 4 days and still in the same amount of pain.	Hopeless, helpless and scared. Beginning to feel depressed.	I'm never going to recover. I'm going to be just like this forever now.	Permanent	It's been going on for 4 days now and nothing the doctors have done has made any difference at all.	Nothing in my life has ever stayed the same forever. Sometimes things have got better, sometimes worse, but nothing has stayed the same.	**Flexible:** Just because it was like this yesterday and is still the same today doesn't mean it will be the same tomorrow. It will get better (great!) or worse (I'll deal with it), but it won't stay the same forever.	Less anxious, and more hopeful. Less, helpless too. Awful depressed feeling lifts.
Standing in a queue, it's moving very slowly. People who arrived at other queues after me are being served before me!	Frustrated and very upset and miserable.	Typical. It's just my luck! There must be something wrong with me. This always happens to me.	Personal Pervasive	I seem to find myself in the slowest queue quite often. Honestly though, I've no idea why this queue is so slow.	If I think about it I can recall times when I've been in the faster queues. What about the other people in the queue, is there something wrong with them too?!	**External:** Other factors like the speed of the server and the needs of others in front affect the speed of the queue. **Specific:** Like other people, sometimes you're in the slow queue and sometimes not.	Much less unhappy. A bit impatient but I don't feel bad about myself.

The examples we've used here come from our own personal experiences and reflect a real process of transition from Three Ps thinking to more realistic thoughts and the resulting changes in emotion. You could just do all of this in your head, but the effect is much more powerful if you write the stages down as you go through them. Also, you can go back through your journal from time to time to remind yourself of how you've taken control of your attitude and the difference that made. This will reinforce the effect further and motivate you to keep doing it.

We've printed a blank journal below for you to fill in if you would like to try this strategy. Ideally though, jot the headings down in a notebook that you can keep close to you all the time. Then you can fill it in when things are actually happening to you. Even when nothing particular is happening, you might find yourself feeling anxious or angry or low. Notice what you are thinking at the time about yourself, other people or your life, and work through the columns. Be aware of how your feelings change as you recognize your style of thinking and challenge and change those thoughts so that they are more realistic and resourceful. If you like, you could also write down the outcomes when those become clear. For example, a week after my original notes on that moment in hospital I could record that the pain did indeed subside and I went home a few days later. This would provide me with further evidence against future permanent kinds of thoughts.

If it isn't possible to work on your journal through the day then you'll need to keep a mental note or just scribble something down on a piece of paper as things occur to you. Then you can fill in your journal fully when it's convenient. It may be that by the time you get to your journal you will be able to write down the eventual outcome and use that when you evaluate your inner voice in the future.

Situation	How Do I Feel, What Do I Do?	What Am I Thinking?	What Thinking Style Is This?	Evidence To Support The Thought	Evidence Against The Thought	Alternative, More Realistic & Helpful Thinking Style	How Do I Feel, What Do I Do?

More than the Three Ps

CBT tends to focus on the Three Ps types of thinking. That's because these are the three that seem to underlie depression and CBT is very often used to treat depression. However, they are not the only kinds of thoughts that can be harmful or undermining.

Remember, evolution has programmed the inner voice to keep people away from danger and draw them back to safe and familiar territory – back to their 'comfort zone'. It is possible to see that this cautionary instinct of the inner voice was once protective and helpful. However, life is different now. The instinct for caution can be a handicap when individuals really want to stretch themselves by leaving their comfort zone and trying something challenging and different. It can especially be a handicap when it goes into overdrive and brings about phobic or panic reactions to things that are actually quite harmless – or at least less harmful than you think when you look at the evidence.

For example, when someone has a flying phobia, what is their inner voice telling them? It's telling them that, if they fly, their plane will crash. But, when you look at the statistics you'll find that the chances of having a crash in a plane are very small indeed. You're much more likely to have a fatal accident out on the road. Yet, people who are terrified of getting onto a plane are quite happy to get into cars or walk across roads, or weave in and out of traffic on bicycles or motorbikes in the centre of big cities without giving much thought to the risks. They'll do all of that, but they won't fly.

Here's another example: people very often describe themselves as 'terrified' of giving public speeches. Their inner voice is warning them that they will make a fool of themselves, that they'll do it so badly they'll be sure to lose everyone's approval. You now know that this is one of the most profound instinctive causes of stress – they'll be humiliated and cast out by the tribe to die in the wilderness alone! They certainly feel and behave as if that's the case. Well, imagine it was you in this situation. In reality what's the worst that could happen? You'll prepare, speak from your heart and give it your best shot. If the audience likes it, that will be great. If they don't, you'll deal with it. You certainly won't die as a result. In any case, once you are committed to doing something that challenges your confidence, you can either tell yourself that you'll fail and it will be a disaster or that you have all the knowledge, skill and ability you need to succeed and you'll be fine. Which of these attitudes do you think will enable you to do well? Obviously, the latter.

As we've said, it takes time and effort to challenge your inner voice and to keep records in this CBT way. But, it's precisely the effort that makes this such an effective strategy. That's because it is effort and involvement in a process that enables deeply embedded learning and change at a profound level. So, if you're up for it, this is a strategy that works to release you from self-critical, self-limiting and undermining thoughts and feelings. It is a strategy that enables you to make a choice about your attitude in a way that can make the difference between stress and resilience and even between depression and mental health. It can make the difference between success and failure, between staying on the ground and in your comfort zone, or taking off, flying to new places and taking on new and exciting challenges. So we would say it's worth it. Would you?

Controlling your inner voice – 2

Use the creativity of your mind

At this point on our courses people often ask us how they can silence their inner voice or change what it says when they've been through the evaluation process and decided that it is saying something unhelpful or unrealistic.

Well, the detailed analysis of the journal is often enough to transform the quality and content of the things that your inner voice tells you. Once you have gathered sufficient evidence to contradict your unhelpful and unrealistic inner voice it simply fades away and you are left with the one that tells you what you really need to hear. However, sometimes the voice can be quite persistent and you find yourself hearing it even though you know it isn't saying anything worth listening to. The voice can be especially difficult to shift if you have been thinking along the same kinds of negative or unrealistic lines for many years. In this case you need an additional set of tools and techniques to act on the voice more directly. For these tools and techniques we turn to another form of therapy called Neuro-Linguistic Programming (NLP). You may be familiar with this approach as it is widely used in the field of popular psychology and personal development, as well as in individual psychotherapy.

NLP shows you how to take control of and transform your inner voice by using the creativity of your mind. There are a great many examples of possible techniques that you could use and it is beyond the scope of our book to go into all of these in detail. (Also, we should note here that you don't only generate voices. You also produce movies, photographs, smells and sensations in your mind. NLP works with all of these, but for this KEY we will focus on the voice that you create). Again, you will find a title in our bibliography if you would like to explore this further. We will give you a very condensed version here that we hope will be sufficient to get you started and enable you to begin to create some of your own techniques.

So, here's a very brief summary of the theory behind NLP transformations in a nutshell:

1 There are certain mental processes involved in creating damaging patterns of thinking.

And:

2 You can use the same mental processes to create more realistic, helpful and even healing patterns of thinking.

Let's look at what all that means.

When you hear a voice in your head, there isn't a real person standing next to you and talking to you. You have generated that voice yourself. If you think about it, it is actually an amazing feat of creativity to bring about something that doesn't actually exist in a concrete way, but that sounds and seems so real that it can have an immediate and powerful effect on how you feel and what you do.

NLP says that it takes certain mental processes to bring about a voice that tells you things that are unrealistic and potentially damaging to your well-being. Since the voice isn't real, it is just a result of mental processes, you can use the same processes to silence that voice and create one that tells you something worth listening to instead.

You'll understand what we mean if you give these techniques a try:

1 In a moment, close your eyes and listen to what your inner voice is saying. Imagine the voice is coming from a radio. Then turn the volume down until the voice is silent or you can just barely hear it. Then, turn it up again so the volume is the same as before. Then open your eyes.

2 Close your eyes and do the same things again, only this time when you turn the volume up make sure your voice is talking about a different subject. Or, you could imagine that you just switch radio channels and begin to listen to a different programme. Then open your eyes.

3 Close your eyes and listen to what your inner voice is saying. Then, in any way you can, imagine you are pushing the voice away from you, way into the distance so it gets quieter and quieter. Then pull it back towards you so it gets louder and louder (you choose whether it is talking about the same thing or something different when it comes back).

When you changed the volume of the voice and the content of its message, you may have found that the sound of the voice changed too. It may have become higher pitched or lower, stronger or more gentle. It may even have become the voice of a different person. That can happen automatically, or you can make it happen deliberately. If you hear the voice of someone whom you fear or dislike, you can turn it into the voice of someone you feel more comfortable with as well as changing the message. If you find it difficult to change the message right away, you could try this: when you close your eyes, turn your inner voice into the voice of your favourite cartoon character and notice how you feel when you do that.

CASE STUDY

I've used this technique many times with patients and clients. I remember a man who had finished a relationship with a woman who had bullied him. Although she was no longer around physically, her harsh and critical voice was still there in his head. He found this disturbing and felt his confidence continuing to be undermined.

He understood that, since she wasn't actually there, he himself created this voice and what it said. He realised he could use this creativity to produce a voice that he could live with more easily instead. First, he changed the voice so it sounded like the cartoon character Betty Boop. I could see him smile when he did this. Then he pushed the voice away until it was so small and weak that eventually he had to strain to hear it. As he pulled the voice back towards him, he turned it into the voice of his best friend reminding him of his great qualities. He did this every time his ex-girlfriend's voice came into his head until she stopped bothering him altogether. As he transformed the voice he transformed his attitude towards himself and allowed his confidence to grow again.

The point is that none of the voices you hear in your head is real. They are all created out of your imagination. So you might as well create a voice that is easy to listen to and that tells you something rational, meaningful and useful.

Exercise fifteen

When you use NLP techniques such as those we've described, your aim is to transform your inner voice once you have decided it is not saying something worth listening to. We've given you some sample techniques to try out to transform your inner voice. Your creative challenge is to come up with some more possible techniques to quieten the voice so it becomes easy to ignore, change the sound of the voice or change what it is saying to you. Here are a few more ideas to get you started:

- Imagine the voice is coming from a yapping dog. Tie the dog to a tree by its lead and walk away from it.

- Imagine the voice is coming from another person. Walk out of the room and close the door.

- When children don't want to listen to something they put their fingers in their ears and sing 'la la lala la, I'm not listening' (very infuriating!). Imagine yourself doing that.

Now, over to you. Write down two or three more, and perhaps even give them a try.

....

....

....

....

....

....

....

....

....

Reflect

We hope you enjoyed those few moments of creativity and thought of some techniques that would work for you. The most important thing to say now is that this is just the start. Reading about NLP and writing some ideas down doesn't make the difference. Doing it makes the difference. The book about NLP that you'll find in our bibliography is called *Use Your Brain For A Change*. The first chapter in that book is titled 'Who's Driving The Bus?' Put your favourite techniques into practice and make sure it's you.

Controlling your inner voice – 3

If you can't make it, fake it

We've presented to you the most widely used strategies and techniques from the kinds of psychotherapy and personal development approaches that have been shown (there is evidence!) to be most effective in reducing stress and depression, and enhancing resilience. We hope very much that you'll give them a go if you become aware that you are adopting an attitude that is 'irrational' and is leading you to feel unnecessarily afraid, unhappy or depressed.

We're also aware that people's attitudes can be very deeply ingrained through years of repetition of the same kinds of interpretations and judgements, and it can take some time and practice before old thinking styles are shifted and new ones are embedded in their place. So we realize that you might find yourself struggling at times to get your mind to think about something in a different way. If that happens, there is another strategy you can use while you practise changing your thoughts in the ways we've discussed.

Do you remember when we discussed the definition of 'attitude' we said that there were two aspects to this? One was that 'attitude' is a person's state of mind with regard to an event, person or object. It's what they think or believe about something. We said that you can change the way you feel by changing the way you think, and that's what we've been working on up till now. But, we also said that 'attitude' is a person's physical posture, facial expression, and the way they communicate. So it is a person's thoughts, but it is also their behaviour. We said that there was a link between these two elements of 'attitude' and it is this:

You can change the way you feel by changing the way you think

AND

You can change the way you think by changing the way you behave.

If you find it difficult to change the way you think about something, simply change the way you behave. In other words, fake it. Even if, after trying out all the CBT and NLP strategies, you still think that everything is terrible and will never get better and it's all your fault, just act *as if* you have a different and more constructive attitude. When you do that it is quite likely that a change in your thoughts will follow.

Exercise sixteen

Try this little experiment.

First, sit down and look at the floor. Allow your head to hang and your shoulders to droop. Let the muscles in your tummy go slack. Furrow your brow a little. Turn the corners of your mouth slightly down. Imagine what the expression in your eyes is when you are feeling low or anxious and deliberately bring that expression about. Stay there for a few minutes and make a mental note of how you feel while you are in this position.

Then, stand up and lift your chin just a little so that you are looking upwards but are able to keep the back of your neck quite long and open. Feel your shoulders relax down and your chest expand slightly. Pull in the muscles of your tummy a little, as though you were trying gently to pull your navel towards your spine. Allow the muscles in your forehead to flatten out so that the space between your eyebrows is smooth. Turn the corners of your mouth slightly up. Imagine what the expression in your eyes is when you are feeling up and confident, and bring that expression about. Again, stay there for a short while and make a mental note of how you feel while you are in this position.

Reflect

What did it feel like to take up each of these two postures?

Of course, we don't know how you would respond to that question. However, from our experience we would expect that you felt a slight pressure of low mood and perhaps even found some worrying thoughts entering into your mind when you looked down, slumped your body and frowned. On the other hand, when you looked up, expanded your chest and relaxed your shoulders and forehead, it is likely that you actually felt more confident and uplifted in your spirits. Perhaps you even had more positive and optimistic thoughts too; you changed your inner voice by changing your physical attitude.

If you did find that you were aware of this difference, you've just given yourself first-hand experience of the power you have to take direct control of the way you feel by changing the way you behave.

There is a perfectly sound scientific explanation for this. Researchers have analysed how different behaviours affect the chemicals in the brain. They've found, for example, that if a person who is not happy acts as if they were happy and smiles, the brain responds by releasing the chemicals that cause a person to feel good for real.

Here's how it works. Your usual experience is that you have positive thoughts, you feel good, and that makes you smile – in that order. But it also works the other way round. When you smile, that makes you feel good! When you feel good your inner voice will reflect more optimistic and hopeful thoughts.

It's the same with confidence. Usually you experience positive and encouraging thoughts first; you feel confident as a result and that leads you to stand up, look up and open your chest. We hope the exercise demonstrated to you that when you stand up, look up and open your chest, this in itself will make you feel happy and confident. Your inner voice will soon follow the trend.

Can you see how that might also apply to the language you use when you communicate with others? Or even when you talk out loud to yourself? If you speak about something being a 'problem' or a 'disaster' then your brain will immediately release chemicals that lead you to feel anxious and overwhelmed (stressed), or even hopeless and helpless (vulnerable to depression). But, if you refer to the same issue as a 'challenge' or 'stretching', then your brain will release chemicals that lead you to feel stimulated and in control. Serotonin is the major chemical that produces these feelings and this is the primary chemical involved in anti-depressant medication. We've put some more of these contrasting words in the table below. Feel free to add any others you can think of on either side to clarify for yourself the difference that the way you use words and language can make to how you feel.

Words That Lead To Stress	Words That Lead To Stimulation
Problem	Challenge
Obstacle	Stimulating
Nuisance	Potential
Handicap	Exciting
Disaster	Novel
Impossible	Different
Catastrophe	Stretching
Depressing	New start
Frightening	Opportunity

At one time a technique called 'autosuggestion' was popular. Autosuggestion was first used as a treatment by the French apothecary Emile Coué in the late 19th century. Coué believed in the effects of his medications. But he also believed that a person's mental state would affect, and could enhance, the effects of those medications. He worked to change the way people thought and felt by changing the way they behaved. Instead of talking about how ill they were and how they would never get better, Coué got them to stand in front of a mirror every day and repeat these words out loud, 'Every day, in every way, I'm getting better and better.' In this he was very much ahead of his time as, of course, at the time there was no technology to view how behaviour affects brain chemicals. He found that this positive self-talk enhanced the effects of his medications, and his discovery was used to support the use of autosuggestion in psychotherapy and personal development through the mid-20th century.

It seems to have fallen out of favour now, probably because people feel a bit embarrassed and awkward if they look in a mirror and talk to themselves. This is most likely to be because of the old saying that 'talking to yourself is the first sign of insanity'. Well, we believe that talking to yourself is the first sign of sanity, as long as you make sure that what you tell yourself is rational and constructive, helpful and healing.

In a challenging situation try this (yes, out loud, in front of a mirror!): 'This situation is here whether I like it or not, and my challenge now is to find the potential and make the best of it. With my inner resources of strength, determination, persistence (or any others that you recognize in yourself) I will find the best possible outcome.'

So now you have the three main ways in which you can change your attitude by taking control of your inner voice. We know that none of these is necessarily going to be easy.

Sometimes this will be because old patterns and habits are deeply ingrained. Sometimes it will be because the situation you are in is especially challenging. In fact, people on our courses often say that it's all very well for us to come in and talk about attitude, but their lives are really tough!

In response we tell them about a man called Viktor Frankl. Frankl survived the Nazi concentration camps and later wrote about his time there (you'll find his book in our bibliography). Frankl was interested in the difference between those who were completely broken by their experiences in the camps and those who displayed extraordinary resilience and came through reasonably intact psychologically and emotionally. He decided the crucial difference was attitude. If attitude made so much difference for people in such dire circumstances, there must be very few times when you would be unable to use it to make the difference for you.

Now, it is extremely important to avoid taking a personal attitude when you find life difficult to handle. We certainly don't want you to start to believe that things are tough because you don't have the 'right attitude'. Life can be very difficult at times. There would be no kind of attitude that could make the experience of a concentration camp easy. There is no kind of attitude that can make being ill easy; or being made redundant, or losing a loved one. Your attitude about what is happening doesn't change what is happening. But it can change how well you are able to cope, recover, and become yourself again. It can give you the precious and powerful quality of resilience.

Attitude makes all the difference

- Your 'attitude' is what you think or believe about something. Attitude is important because the way you think affects the way you feel. You always have the ability to choose your attitude.

- Beware of faulty thinking styles that create vulnerability to stress. These are the 'Three Ps': believing that setbacks are Permanent, Pervasive and Personal. Cognitive Behavioural Therapy offers more rational thinking styles: Flexible, Specific and External.

- You can change the way you think by transforming your inner voice. Ensure that it communicates more realistically positive messages to you and positive feelings will follow. Positive feelings will lead to more positive outcomes.

- Your attitude doesn't change what is happening in your life. But it can change how well you are able to cope and to recover from setbacks. This is the quality of resilience.

Everything can be taken from a man but one thing: the last of the human freedoms – to choose one's attitude in any given set of circumstances, to choose one's own way.

VIKTOR FRANKL

KEY 7

12

Live in the present

Pain and anxiety come from reliving the past or imagining the future. Focus on the present moment. It's the only one that's real.

This final KEY emerges from ideas you are already familiar with from the previous chapters. So we expect you will probably find this the easiest of the 7 KEYS to grasp and your journey should be an easy downhill ride from here.

The point is simple. We believe that most of the stress people experience does not arise as a result of things that are happening to them in the immediate present moment. It does sometimes, of course. For example, someone's life might be threatened. Even if an event in the present moment isn't actually life-threatening, it is still possible that other kinds of severe consequences could arise unless immediate action is taken. This happens fairly frequently for some people; for example, for those who engage in high-risk activities, or who work in emergency or police services. But, for most people, such emergencies happen extremely rarely. The stress that most people feel, most of the time, comes not from what is happening to them or to others in the present moment, but from a different place and time.

Stress comes from the past and the future

We think that most of people's stress and anxiety comes about as a result of their reflections on the past or projections into the future.

Here's the theory...

If you think about the nature of 'the past' and 'the future', you will see right away that both of these are beyond a person's ability to control. The past is gone and it is not possible to change it. You can't go back and do or say things differently. And, the future hasn't happened yet. We've looked at ways in which you can prepare and plan for future change so that you can be in control as much as possible. For the most part though, you can't know everything about what will happen and it is not possible to control what you don't know and can't predict. So people can't control the past or the future.

But, as we've said (repeatedly!) throughout this book, people need to be in control and that need for control is profound and instinctive. So people find it very difficult to 'let go'. They ponder and ruminate on the past and the future because that gives them a feeling of control. The past and future seem still to be within their grasp as long as they hang on to their thoughts and imaginings.

However, the reality is of course that this sense of control is an illusion. The past will always be as it was and there is nothing you can do to change it. The future is largely unpredictable and there will always be things that you will have to deal with as they arise. So, in fact, rather than easing stress by maintaining control, thinking about the past and the future actually increases stress because the control isn't real!

Rather than trying to gain control of times and events that are out of your control, we would like to encourage you to focus on the one moment in which you always have absolute control of everything you do, feel and think. The moment you are in right now. The present.

Exercise seventeen

Awareness is the first step to achieving the aim of this KEY. Take some time now to discover how often you are engaged fully in the present moment, and what it feels like when you achieve that state of mind.

This is an exercise we are not able to ask people to do in our live presentations. That's because it takes the form of an experiment you will run on yourself over the course of a few days. In our live sessions we have to ask people just to reflect and remember how they spend their time. You will be able to monitor it for real and so your results will be much more accurate.

For this experiment you need to:

1 Copy the table below onto sheets of paper that you can easily carry with you, in a notebook for example.

Date & Time	What am I doing?	What am I thinking?	How do I feel? S (1–10) H (1–10)

2 Set an alarm clock or an alert on your mobile phone (again use something that you can have with you all the time) to ring in two hours' time.

3 Carry on with your life as usual.

4 When the signal comes, stop what you are doing for a few moments. Quickly make brief entries under the headings in your table. Under 'What am I thinking?' jot down your thoughts and then in brackets say whether your focus is on the future, the past or the present.

When you get to the 'How do I feel?' column you can write comments, or you might like to use a numerical scale to make it simpler. At the top of that column we've suggested two scales; a stress/calm scale S (1–10) where 1 is extremely stressed and 10 is absolutely calm, and an unhappy/happy scale H (1–10) where 1 is extremely unhappy and 10 is joyfully happy.

I've put in my own entries for this moment as an example below. My mind is entirely focused on what I am doing right now so I am definitely in the present moment. I feel quite calm (S8) and neither very happy nor very unhappy. I feel simply content (H5).

Notice how short and to-the-point the entries are. You have plenty of other things to do (I have to get on with writing!) so spend only a few moments on this each time.

Date & Time	What am I doing?	What am I thinking?	How do I feel? S (1–10) H (1–10)
20th June 13.30pm	Writing this book	Concentrating on the best way to explain the exercise (present)	S 8 H 5

5 Reset your alarm for a different time period. We would suggest no less than half an hour and no more than two hours. So you could set it to ring again in 40 minutes, or an hour and a half, etc.

6 Repeat instructions 3 to 5.

We'd like you to do this for at least two days. If you work, it would be best to include both working and leisure days so you cover the widest possible range of times and places for your experiment.

As well as writing in your table when your alarms ring, please also add entries just before you are about to go to sleep. If you wake up in the night and struggle to get back to sleep, then write this down in your table and record your thoughts and feelings (as well as providing you with valuable information for the experiment it may also help you to go back to sleep).

Whether you set an alarm to wake you in the morning or just let yourself wake up naturally, let this be the time for your first notes of the day.

Finally, resist the temptation to look back and review your entries. Once you have written down all you need for a particular moment in time put the table away. When the alarm sounds again, just start writing immediately without looking back over previous entries.

Now you are ready to start. Put this book away until you have finished your experiment. Your alarm will go off in 2 hours...

Welcome back. Now take a look through the entries you have made over the last couple of days. What sorts of activities and thoughts are linked with your happiest and calmest scores or reports?

Reflect

In a scientific journal (*Science*, Nov 2010) two researchers called Matthew Killingsworth and Daniel Gilbert wrote about an experiment very similar to the one you have just carried out (in our bibliography there is also a book by Daniel Gilbert called *Stumbling on Happiness* that you might find interesting). These researchers used an iPhone app to interrupt thousands of people repeatedly during the course of their everyday lives and got them to report on what they were doing and how they were feeling at that time. Killingsworth and Gilbert found two things:

1 people think about what is not happening almost as often as they think about what is;

and

2 thinking about what is not happening usually makes people unhappy.

We expect you will have found the same for yourself. When your own alarm sounded we expect you will often have been thinking about something other than what you were doing or what was actually happening in that moment. Also, we imagine you will have found that any feelings of stress and unhappiness were linked mostly with the times when you were brooding on the past or imagining the future.

Eckhart Tolle puts it like this:

Unease, anxiety, tension, stress, worry – all forms of fear – are caused by *too much future*, and not enough present. Guilt, regret, resentment, grievances, sadness, bitterness... are caused by *too much past*, and not enough present.

Your moments of peace and happiness were most likely to be related to times when you were fully engaged or absorbed in the activity or experience of the moment. That's because, as we've said, people are very rarely stressed by something that is happening during the moment they are in. Whatever threatened you in the past or you fear will threaten you in the future, none of it is happening *right now*. Right now, in this second, you are alive and have the opportunity to react constructively to the past, make the most of the present and prepare for the future in any way you like. In this moment you can take complete control.

Learn to live in the present

Of all our KEYS, this is probably the easiest to agree with. It's really obvious when you think about it. However, although it is very easy to agree with, it can be very difficult to do. The tendency to think so frequently about the past and the future will by now be a habit formed over many years, and it can be hard work and take time to 'unlearn' such a deeply ingrained pattern. Let's have a look at some of the techniques and strategies you might use to help you to break a habit that gives you an illusion of control and develop one that gives you real control; one that brings with it a deep sense of peace and even pleasure.

Learning to live in the present – 1

Interrupt yourself

The experiment you worked through in the last exercise is actually a well-known technique that you can continue to use to develop the habit of living in the present. When your alarm or alert signals a break, this interrupts your ruminations and reflections on the past and future and reminds you to focus on the here-and-now. You could think of it as being distracted from your distractions. If you keep doing this for a while you will find that, more and more often, when your alarm sounds, you are already in the present.

Learning to live in the present – 2

Mindfulness meditation

Throughout the centuries, the search for a state of 'inner peace' has led people to experience and appreciate the power and value of meditation. Many people dismiss meditation as something they could never do because they 'would never be able to empty their minds and not think about things'. Well, it would be a shame to miss out on the benefits of this ancient technique for this reason, because that's not what meditation is about. No one can 'empty their mind and not think about anything'. That's not how the mind works.

Your thoughts are the result of electrical currents constantly stimulating billions of nerve cells in your brain, and it is completely impossible to stop this. Whether or not the nerve cells in your brain are activated is something that is out of your control.

So, you can't control *that* you think. *But*, as the previous KEYS have shown, you have absolute control over *what* you think.

Meditation doesn't ask you to think about nothing. It simply asks you to think about less. As Michael Yapko (another author you met earlier in this book) would say, to meditate is to 'focus more and more on less and less'.

When you meditate you channel that unstoppable electrical energy. Instead of allowing it to flit around all sorts of clutter about the past and the future, you gradually, deliberately, bring your focus to one thing. You don't empty your mind. You fill it... with less. That's mindfulness.

Now, of course, you could choose to fill your mind with thoughts of the past or future. That would be a form of meditation. But we hope we've convinced you that you are most likely to experience ease and contentment when you are completely engaged with the present. Meditations that are focused in the present moment take many different forms. People who practise regularly become very skilled at letting go of the disturbing distractions of past and future. They might concentrate instead on their moment-by-moment experience of themselves and how they feel physically or emotionally. Or, they may focus on more universal issues such as suffering and compassion.

If you are already experienced in meditation then we're sure you feel the benefit and would simply encourage you to continue to keep practising and developing that skill. For those who are just starting out, here is an exercise you can use to begin to train your mind to focus more and more on less and less.

This exercise is based on a simple meditation devised by Jon Kabat-Zinn who has written many books and carried out a great deal of research on how mindfulness can be used in clinical applications for stress-related disorders.

Exercise eighteen

It would be ideal if you could get someone to read through these steps while you practise them, or perhaps you could make a recording as you read them aloud and then play it back to yourself. If neither of these is possible then just read through the whole exercise and have a go. It's a simple technique and easy to remember.

1   To begin, just for a few moments, become very aware of all of your thoughts as they come and go.

2   Take a couple of deep breaths. Concentrate on your out-breath. When you breathe out deliberately in this way you are signalling to the body that you no longer need extra oxygen to fuel fight-or-flight and that it is ok to relax.

3   Open your eyes very wide and look all around you. Look up and around, down and around, to each side and in front and behind you. Consciously register all of the objects around you and any colours or light and shade you can see.

4   Lower your eyelids and listen very carefully to all the sounds that you can hear. First, focus on sounds coming from a distance, then on the sounds closer to you.

5   Now become very aware of everything you can feel on the outside of your body. Notice any sensations on your skin such as warmth or coolness, the weight and texture of the material of your clothes, any part of your body that is resting on support behind your back or underneath you.

6   Now become very aware of everything you can feel inside your body. Become aware of any shifts, movements or sensations happening inside your body.

7   One of the things that can be most noticeable when you focus on your body in this way is the process of breathing. Focus on that for a while. Become very aware of how you are breathing, and what it feels like to be breathing. Concentrate entirely on the act of breathing. Experience the cooling sensation as air passes through the nostrils, feel the air slowly moving in and out of the lungs, listen to the sound of the air movement. Allow these sensations to exclude all other distractions.

8   Keep your focus on the breath for as long as you are comfortable. Remember that the mind has a natural tendency to wander. Let thoughts drift into your awareness, then just let them drift out again without judging or evaluating them, and without attempting to problem-solve. Imagine they are like waves washing onto a beach and then being pulled away again back out to sea. Let the thoughts come, let them go, and gently bring your focus back to the breath.

With practice you will find that your focus on the breath will be more complete for longer periods of time.

9   When you feel ready you can begin to reverse the process. Now you start to focus more and more on more and more again. Become aware again of the whole of the inside of your body... the outside of your body... the sounds that you can hear coming from close by... the sounds that you can hear coming from a distance. Raise your eyelids again and look around again.

10   Take a couple of deep breaths again (your breathing will probably have become quite shallow during the meditation so deep breaths will replenish oxygen) and stretch and move your body to re-energize yourself.

Reflect

When we do this exercise in our groups people's reactions vary from deep engagement and focus to an almost unchanged level of distraction. When people remain disengaged from the meditation process this can be because they are unable to channel the energy of their minds in this way or, for a number of possible reasons, simply do not wish to. This is fine. If you found yourself in this category you are not bad or wrong. Meditation is not for everyone. We hope the other strategies we cover to enable focus on the present moment will be more useful to you. If you did go along with the process, here are a few questions and thoughts to reflect on.

What was it like?

Most people say that it is a very pleasant experience. It reminds them how rarely they do just sit quietly and still, and what a relief it can be to take a break from all the physical and mental 'rushing around'.

What did you notice about what you were aware of as you shifted your attention from one thing to another?

In Part One of this book we reflected on how amazing the frontal cortex of the human brain is in its ability to analyse, interpret, create and calculate. And this is true, it is amazing. The scope of the human brain is immense. Yet, in one crucial way it is extremely limited. It can only be fully and attentively conscious of one thing at a time.

It isn't possible, for example, to have a conversation with someone and do another task at the same time. You can share your attention between the two, but both cannot have your full attention (think about what this means in relation to the concept of multi-tasking). It isn't possible to listen intently to a discussion on the radio and watch a television programme with equal attention at the same time. If you are busy with something and someone calls you, you experience that as a distraction because you have to stop what you are doing to respond. You can only think about one thing at a time. Sometimes it may feel as though you have a lot of things on your mind all at once, but this is just because one thought is following another very quickly. You are still only thinking about one thing at a time.

For this reason, it is most likely that you were hardly aware of any physical sensations when you were listening to the sounds around you, and then barely aware of any sounds when you turned your attention to your body. After this, when you focused just on your breath, you probably weren't aware of much else. The physical sensations and sounds that were so prominent when you were actively observing them will have all but disappeared. Any thoughts that drifted into your mind will have taken your attention away from the breath for a moment, but then those thoughts will have been pushed away when you refocused.

This limit of conscious awareness can be frustrating. It would be great to be able to work and have a conversation and respond to your child's needs with equal attention all at the same time! However, this limiting factor is a vital survival mechanism. In an emergency, you need to be able to maintain complete focus on the present moment. For your purposes in building resilience, it is also a gift. It is this limit that makes it possible to think more and more about less and less. If you really immerse yourself in thinking about just one thing it is simply not possible for thoughts about anything else to enter your awareness at the same time. This is what makes it possible to live simply and fully in the present moment whenever you choose to do so.

How did you feel as you focused just on the act of breathing?

People we work with who do engage with this process tell us they felt deeply relaxed at the point of focus on the breath. This is great and we hope you experienced that too. With the focus on the breath there is no past and no future to disturb or concern you. Keeping your mind so intensely focused within the present moment in this way can bring a wonderful sense of stillness and peace.

How did you feel when you brought everything back into your conscious awareness? What kinds of thoughts did you have then? What did you want to do?

People say that they still maintain some of that sense of deep relaxation when they come out of their focused state. Thoughts begin to come into their minds again but not as frantically as before and without worry or anxiety attached. Rather than being drawn into ruminations about the past or the future, their initial thoughts seem to be much more about what is happening to them right now. For a brief moment their mind has been trained to focus on the here-and-now and they feel ready to live in the present moment more calmly and purposefully. We wonder if you found the same, and hope that you did.

Mindfulness meditation can be a valuable process in itself in that it can give you a moment to rest and recover when you are under pressure or going through a difficult time. As a tool to build resilience, though, it is really a means to a different end. That is to be able to focus on the present moment more and more easily and often in your everyday life.

Every time you use a technique like this the effect of each practice builds on the last. It is like training muscles to become fit and strong. Each visit to the gym has a small, barely noticeable effect. But, little bit by little bit, over time, strength and fitness grow until you get to a point where you can do things you couldn't do before with little or no effort. In the same way, each meditation practice builds and reinforces your 'resilience muscles'. Gradually your ability to keep your mind on what is happening right now will grow until, eventually, you will find that you are doing that without even trying.

CASE STUDY

One of the most common complaints we hear from people who attend our sessions is that they have difficulty sleeping. When they go to bed they find it hard to switch off from the pressures and demands of their lives and their rest is constantly disrupted by thoughts. Of course, these thoughts are not about what is happening in the present moment. In the present moment nothing is happening. They are just lying there trying to get to sleep! The thoughts that churn around their heads and disturb them as they lie there are about the past or the future. They are about things that are not happening. Most people are prone to this kind of experience from time to time and I am no exception.

Here is my two-part strategy for getting to sleep.

1   I sit up (sometimes I even get up and go into a different room) and I write down any thoughts I have had that I need to remember, or any actions that I need to take. If I am worrying about something I can have no control over, I think about KEYS 1 and 5. I let go and trust myself to be able to deal with whatever happens. If there is something I can control but don't have a solution or action, I write down the worry and also give myself a time slot the next day to have that worry. (Worries are like children, if you try to ignore them they just shout more loudly. So there is no point telling yourself 'don't worry' and trying to ignore your concerns, they'll just shout more loudly. If you acknowledge your concerns and make an appointment to pay attention at a better time then they will quieten down). Making notes like this gives me a sense of control and that prevents the build up of stress overnight.

2   Once I feel more in control I embark on the mindfulness meditation. This pushes all thoughts of past and future out of my mind and I am focused on the present moment. In that moment there is nothing happening and nothing I can do about anything that has happened or will happen. I usually fall asleep at Step 4 of the meditation when I become aware of the feeling of the weight of my head on the pillows, my body sinking into the mattress and the softness and warmth of the duvet....

We just said that using techniques such as the mindfulness meditation to develop the ability to live in the present is like training for fitness and strength in the gym. But what if you don't like going to the gym? Do you have to stay weak and unfit? No, of course not. There are lots of different ways to achieve the same effect. You could swim, run, cycle, walk, dance, play a sport, dig the garden (I just heard someone on the radio say they'd cancelled their gym membership after they started working on an allotment. She said, 'Have you ever felt your stomach muscles after digging in the garden for a morning?'). Any kind of activity that involves moving around with some degree of effort will have a similar effect.

In the same way, if sitting still and entering into a focused meditation is not something you feel comfortable with or enjoy, there are many other ways to achieve the same effect. Our third strategy for learning to live in the present is one of these.

Learning to live in the present – 3

Experience flow

Go back for a moment to the table or notebook you kept for Exercise Seventeen. Look down the right-hand column and find those entries that produced scores low on stress and around the middle mark or higher for happiness. Actually, the example I gave of a moment of writing about the exercise is one of those. At that instant I felt very calm so I scored my stress/calm scale at 8. I couldn't say it was 10 and I guess that's because there's always an element of hope of approval and sense of lack of control when you write something for other people to read. You want them to like it but can't be absolutely sure that they will. I gave myself a score of 5 for happiness. I was feeling neither very happy nor very unhappy. I just *was*. I felt ok. I felt quite content and at peace inside myself. Do you have any entries similar to this?

If you do, you have experienced something that a Hungarian professor of psychology called Mihaly Csikszentmihalyi named 'flow'. People experience flow when they are immersed in tasks that they find interesting, pleasurable and fulfilling. According to Csikszentmihalyi, the state of flow can sometimes

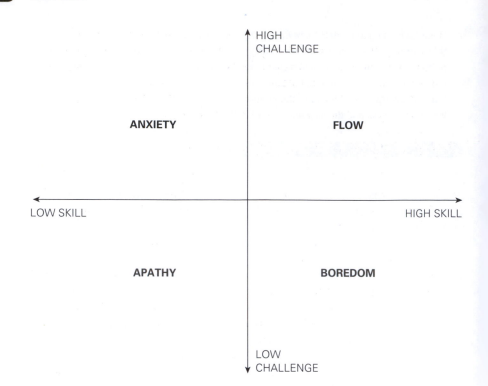

even bring about feelings of 'rapture' and 'joy'. It is like a kind of meditation. All other thoughts are pushed out by your complete absorption in the task at hand. When you are in flow you lose track of time. After what seems like an hour you stop and find that three hours have passed. We could say that in flow you almost go beyond living in the present to a place that is somehow removed from time altogether. This is the most mindful state you can achieve. It is the embodiment of living in the moment, and you don't need formal meditation techniques to get there.

So, what does it take to achieve a state of flow? There are three main requirements. The first two are:

1 you need to be skilled enough to carry out the task;

2 you need to be challenged by the task to a certain extent.

The diagram above illustrates how an activity will fail to generate the condition of flow for you if one of these characteristics is missing.

Here you can see that if an activity is too easy you will become bored, and boredom opens the door to distractions and ruminations that take you away from the present. On the other hand, when you attempt to take on a task for which you don't have sufficient skill, then that is a route to anxiety and stress through lack of control and fear of failure (we find this often comes up as a source of stress for people in the workplace when they are given a job or a task for which they have not been sufficiently well trained). With neither skill nor challenge you would find yourself in the state of apathy. In this state people become devoid of all emotion, purpose or interest and this makes them vulnerable to the hopelessness and helplessness we talked about in relation to depression in KEY 6.

The third main requirement for achieving a state of flow is:

3 you want to do the task as well as you can for its own intrinsic worth, or your own desire to do so, not for financial gain or the approval of others.

As soon as there is an element of judgement from someone else, or the pressure of financial motivation, which, after all, usually relies on the approval of someone else, this has the potential to trigger the stress response and stress will take you out of flow. I had this in a very minor way when writing about the exercise earlier (hence the stress score of 2). But this was insignificant while I was engaged in the process of writing. I simply wanted the work to be as good as it could be for my own satisfaction in producing something of high quality that I could be proud of.

Now you know what flow is you probably recognize that there are things you already do that take you into flow from time to time. If so, build on them, make even more time for them. They are more valuable than you perhaps thought.

If you don't really recognize this as a state that you've experienced very often or at all then we would strongly encourage you to seek ways to bring flow into your life, ideally as part of your daily, habitual routine.

You could do this by cultivating a passion. Pick a subject that fascinates you, study it and immerse yourself in it totally. Engage in an activity that is enjoyable and challenges you. Maybe you won't be in flow immediately. Sometimes it takes time and practice to develop sufficient skill to enable flow. If you can weather the fear of failure at the beginning and keep at it then the experience of flow you eventually achieve will enhance your resilience and enrich your life.

CASE STUDY

When I carried out research for the book *Fast Track to the Top,* I interviewed some of the world's most successful business leaders. I analysed 80 success stories to identify their most effective qualities and strategies. The people who contributed to the book led extremely busy lives. They were so successful because of their strong commitment to their careers.

However, I quickly became struck by the fact that all of them had a serious alternative interest in their lives. The range of these was as diverse as their careers and included photography, sailing, opera, playing music, following sport, painting and, in one case, collecting egg-cups. The participants were extremely knowledgeable and enthusiastic about their particular interests. Through these they had the opportunity to change the pace of their lives and to immerse themselves in the condition of flow whenever they chose.

On the other hand, it isn't only things that you are very passionate about that can take you into a state of flow. You can create it for yourself out of any mundane and ordinary task or job you do every day. In fact, anything you do from brushing your teeth, to eating a meal, to writing a report, to cleaning out the cupboards or painting a wall has the potential to take you into flow. All you need to do is to deliberately focus intently on the task. Do easy things as if they were challenging enough to demand your complete attention. If you bring the focus of all of your senses to a simple daily activity like washing your hands, this can become an absorbing mindful meditation that gives you a few moments of blissful in-the-moment peace during a busy day.

Flow is a powerful antidote to stress, so it is a condition that is worth cultivating wherever and whenever possible. The quality we describe in our next strategy has some aspects that are similar to flow, and can also be a way to induce a state of flow quite spontaneously.

Learning to live in the present – 4

Rediscover your inner curious child

If you think about it, you will probably agree that you were extremely good at living in the present when you were a child. Very young children exist from moment to moment. One of the reasons for this is that, from one moment to the next, they are curious about what is going on. That curiosity leads them to become completely absorbed in whatever they are doing. They have to investigate thoroughly every angle, every smell, taste and texture. They need to know 'what?' and 'how?' and, in particular (and often infuriatingly!) 'why?' They delve into their new world with the kind of focused attention that leads them frequently into a state of blissful flow in which they forget time and place.

Then they start to grow up and begin to accumulate the baggage of life. They learn that there is a time to come which is bigger than the next instant and that things will happen in that 'bigger time': the future. They start to have feelings of dread or happy anticipation of what is to come. As well as getting a sense of the future, the past becomes more real too. Other people's reflections and judgements on past experiences, and the children's own developing memories, bring the past to life in their present. As developing humans, the instinct for control leads children to dwell on the future and the past just as it does for adults. By the time they are adults themselves they hardly exist in the moment at all. Life races on while they are busy reliving the past or ruminating on the future. Does that sound like you?

It wouldn't be surprising at all if you did recognize your own emergence from childhood in this description since it is simply the necessary learning process that all young humans have to go through to be able to function and survive as an adult in the world. But, as you've gathered from KEY 5, you now have all of the skills, qualities, knowledge and experience you need to deal with pretty much anything that comes along. So might it not be possible for you to 'let go' a little and allow yourself to rekindle some of that childhood curiosity?

CASE STUDY

I hope this little diversion doesn't seem too corny but, honestly, when did you last really look at a cloud?

As a passenger on a car journey a little while ago, I was regretting the end of a pleasant holiday and already planning, in slightly anxious anticipation of a busy time ahead. Suddenly I became aware that, while the sky in front was completely clear and bright, above us and to each side there were heavy, black looming clouds. That was suddenly fascinating to me. The weather ahead was bright and sunny and people could have been out sunbathing in their gardens but, just a few miles away to the east and west, it was practically dark. I imagined people there rushing indoors to escape the rain. Then I noticed that, although the clouds were just as black and heavy wherever they hung in the sky, it was actually raining in only some places. It wasn't raining on our car, but just a little way away it was pouring down. I was completely absorbed in watching these clouds and wondering how there could be such a difference in weather in such a little distance, and also why only some of the clouds were producing rain and not all of them. I turned to the driver and said, 'Aren't clouds strange? Why isn't all the cloud raining?' In that brief moment I lived completely in the present, as a child would. The past and future disappeared and I felt perfectly at ease living in the present, which, after all, was exactly where I was and the only place I can ever really be.

To be curious is a matter of choice. As we said in KEY 6, you always have a choice about what you think. You can choose to dwell on the difficulties of the days ahead or a troubling past event, or you can choose to take a curious interest in what is happening around you in the immediate instant.

You can choose to become captivated by the strange shape or beauty or even ugliness of a building, or by the coolness or warmth of the weather, or the immense variety and mystery of the plant and wildlife around you even in the most built-up areas of big towns and cities. Other people are endlessly intriguing. Watch them. Notice how they move, what they are wearing, the expressions on their faces. Listen to whoever speaks to you with close attention. Every individual person has a fascinating story to tell and their own unique way of telling it. Fill your senses with passing aromas. Really savour the tastes and textures of the food. Immerse yourself in the process of eating. These are all things that children do. Watch a child eat an ice-cream. They do it with their whole heart and soul and make it last as long as they can. Watch an adult eat an ice-cream. Three gulps and it's gone. They've hardly noticed the burst of cold and intense flavour before they're hurrying on to the next thing they have to do.

If you can let go of being an adult with a complex past or a demanding future for just a short while every now and again you will bring yourself into a safe, intriguing present and the experience will be rewarding and enriching. It will also work like another trip to the 'resilience gym', enhancing your ability to cope with the next challenge to come along.

And, of course, there will always be challenges. While it can be valuable to let yourself live in the moment in a childlike way every now and again, the fact is you are an adult. You have a past that you need to reconcile and integrate into your current life, and you have a future which you need to plan for to ensure ongoing well-being and security for yourself and your dependants and loved ones. How can you achieve these things while at the same time practising this KEY and living in the present?

Our fifth and final strategy will show you.

Learning to live in the present – 5

Bring the past and the future into the present

In our KEY 2 we talked about how important it is for you to have clear goals and ambitions, and to plan your days to make sure you can spend time on those. In KEY 4 we presented ways to help you to plan for future change. KEY 5 included an exercise that specifically asked you to reflect for a while on a past experience. In our live presentations, people quite often say that these strategies and exercises seem to contradict the idea that they should live in the present moment. We agree. It can seem as though there is a conflict between your need to acknowledge the past and to develop goals and plans for the future, and the value of living in the present.

To resolve this conflict we might look again to Eckhart Tolle who believes strongly in the vital importance of living in the present (he wrote the book, *The Power Of Now* which is in our bibliography). Tolle looks at it this way. Whatever you are thinking about and whatever you are doing, you are doing it now. Since time-travel is not possible (yet...) you are, in reality, always in the present moment. Even though our last four strategies have described ways that you can become more skilled at living in the present, perhaps the most powerful technique you can use is just to realize that you simply always are.

Thinking about the past or the future is only stressful and damaging to your resilience when you allow yourself to react physically or emotionally as though you were actually there. If you immerse yourself in memories in such a way that it is like you are going through unpleasant past experiences all over again this can be painful, distressing, even traumatic. If you project into the future as though you were actually there and living through all of the terrible things you imagine, then this can be frightening and upsetting too (remember our earlier story about killing George?).

Deal with the past, and plan for the future, but always with the conscious recognition that you are doing those things in the present.

Even when you do that, you will probably feel some emotional reaction to your reflections. You are human after all. Emotions are part of being human, and part of being a resilient human. As we've said before, the opposite of stressed isn't 'calm'. It is to feel emotions that are appropriate to the situation that you find yourself in at any time. When you feel the pain of past experiences as if they were happening to you again in the present then that level of pain is not appropriate. If you feel fear and anguish over events you imagine in the future as if those events were actually taking place right now then that level of fear and anguish is not appropriate. None of those things is actually happening to you in the present. In the present instant you are safe and have absolute control of everything you do, feel and think.

However scary or painful your projections into the past and future become, if you keep reminding yourself that you are always and inescapably in the present, you will be in control. When you remember your past you will be able to do that in a way that helps you recognize how all of your experiences have added to your personal qualities and skills, as you did in KEY 5. You will be able to look to the future with a perspective that enables you to review your personal strengths and desires, explore options, and set goals in a structured and strategic way as you did in KEYS 2 and 4.

If you bring your past and future into your present like this then remembering and planning can become in-the-moment acts. They can be absorbing and satisfying in themselves. They may even be routes to the condition of flow.

So, to live in the present, you don't have to push away memories from the past or stop yourself from thinking ahead and making plans. Just do those things from the here and now. It's the only place and time that's real.

We've now explored quite extensively the techniques and strategies you can use to develop your ability to live in the present. We've done that because we know that people's stress arises most often when they are not living in the present, and the aim of this book is to help you to lower stress so your resilience can flourish.

We'd like to finish this chapter with another, perhaps even more compelling reason for you to work towards achieving this KEY. Here we'd like you to recall the central message from KEY 3. Life is short and precious. Maybe the past was better, maybe it was worse than your present life. Maybe the future will be better and maybe it will be worse. That is all immaterial right now, in this moment.

How much of your time do you want to spend in a time and place that doesn't exist any more, or hasn't arrived yet? This is your one life. The past is gone and the future hasn't happened yet. This moment is all there is. Make the most of it.

Live in the present

- People become stressed by ruminating about the past or projecting into the future. But you can't change the past, and the future is largely unpredictable.

- Instead of dwelling on times and events that are out of your control, focus on the moment you are in right now.

- Thinking about the past and the future is a habit formed over many years. To develop the ability to live in the present:

  1 set an alarm to remind you to focus on the here-and-now;

  2 practise a mindfulness meditation;

  3 experience 'flow' – the total absorption in a task;

  4 rekindle your childhood curiosity;

  5 deal with the past and plan for the future with a recognition that you are doing those things in the present.

- This moment is all there is. Make the most of it.

The more you are focused on time – past and future – the more you miss the Now, the most precious thing there is.

ECKHART TOLLE

The last word

Congratulations on completing our 7 KEYS. It's been quite a long journey and we appreciate the effort that you have made along the way. Well done!

In return for your hard work we will give you a promise. We guarantee that whenever you find yourself in a difficult situation and realize that you are becoming stressed, one of these 7 KEYS will always come to your rescue.

There's just one proviso. That is, if you want these KEYS to work for you, you have to keep working on them.

During every course we've presented over the years, someone has always at some point said 'Yes, but that's easier said than done!' As we've said before in this book, and as we say to them, we agree. The KEYS are easier to understand, talk about, and even to agree with, than they are to do. That's because each of them asks you to act against your deeply ingrained habitual patterns and even against your instinct.

But, you know, you really don't need things to be easy in order to do them. Throughout your life you have done things in spite of the fact that they have been hard to do. You've done them anyway because they've been important to you and worth the effort. Yes the KEYS are hard to do, but do them anyway because there aren't many things that are as important as your mental and physical well-being. There are not many qualities as worth building as resilience.

So, the fact that it might be hard for you to put the KEYS into practice is not a reason for not doing it. However, it is a reason to take it easy and not be too hard on yourself while you begin to do things differently.

It might help you to see the process of unlearning deeply embedded habitual behaviours and adopting new ones as taking place over four stages. The origin of this particular model of learning is not exactly known. Some say it was created by an employee of a company called Gordon Training International, others say that's not the case. In any event, we have come across it many times in different teaching environments and it seems to make a lot of sense. It is often called 'The Learning Staircase', or 'The Learning Ladder', and you might have come across it too.

It works like this.

At first you are in a state of 'unconscious incompetence'. This means you don't know that there is something you don't know. For example, before you knew what a car was you didn't know that you couldn't drive one.

Then, you did know what a car was. You wanted to be able to drive but you knew that you didn't know how. At that point you are in a state of 'conscious incompetence'. You are unable to drive and you know it.

So, you start to take lessons. You realize that, although it looked quite easy when you watched an experienced driver, it is actually very difficult. There are many things that you have to do at the same time and this is hard because, as you've seen, your conscious mind can only pay full attention to one thing at a time. Now you are at the stage of 'conscious competence'. You know what you need to do, but because you have to concentrate consciously on each separate action one at a time, your driving is jerky and uncertain, and you make lots of mistakes. You feel uncomfortable and frustrated. You may even find this part of the learning process quite stressful as your need for approval kicks in and you are afraid to look foolish in front of your instructor, and maybe even other road users (who you don't know and will never see again). Also, you feel a sense of lack of control, as you don't yet have the skill to make the car do exactly what you want it to do at the instant and in the way that you choose.

But, even though it is hard, you persevere because you know you will gain great benefits from being able to drive and it is worth it to you. You have more lessons. You get into the car and go through the motions of driving over and over again. Gradually you find that you are able to handle the car, deal with changing conditions on the road, respond to signs and signals and the behaviour of other drivers, and react to emergencies without thinking about every single thing that you do. Now you have reached the point of 'unconscious competence'. You can drive, and you are no longer aware of how you are doing it. You just drive.

It will be the same with the KEYS. Before you picked up this book you were doing things in your life that were unhelpful and maybe even harmful to your resilience and well-being, without knowing it. You were in a state of unconscious incompetence. Then you started reading this book and became aware of those unhelpful patterns of behaviour, why they arose and what you need to do to change. You moved to the state of conscious incompetence.

If you decide to change some of your habitual behaviour by following any of our strategies and techniques, then you will have started your 'driving lessons' and you will be at the level of conscious competence. This is the most uncomfortable stage. You'll feel unnatural, make mistakes and slip back into old patterns sometimes. You'll be frustrated, impatient and maybe even angry with yourself now and again. But, let all of that go. Be patient and gentle with yourself. Stay focused on why you are making the change and what you will gain by doing so. Consciously do it again and again. You can be sure that if you push on and persevere, you will reach that stage of unconscious competence. Your new approach will be part of you. Your new behaviours won't be things that you have to consciously try to do; they will be part of who you are.

And even then, you won't be at the end of the road. You'll still slip back every now and again. I've been doing these KEYS for years and I still sometimes say 'yes' when I want to say 'no'. I still sort e-mails into folders or tidy cupboards when I know there are other things I need to do that are much more important to me. I sometimes feel anxious when things change, and doubt my skills and ability to cope. I tell myself that it's 'typical' when I get stuck in the slowest queue, and if my favourite football team loses I blame myself for watching. I very rarely now get immersed in ruminations about the past to the point where I feel as if I am going through it all over again, but it does happen. And that's ok. It's ok because now I am aware and I know what to do about it. I just have to do it consciously for a while again. I let myself off the hook because I know that at any moment I am doing my best. You will be too.

So, the last word is...

PRACTISE.

Practise, practise, practise, and you will get there.

Thank you for your company, and good luck!

REFERENCES AND FURTHER READING

Aurelius, M (1997) *Meditations*, trans Robin Hard, Wordsworth Editions Ltd, Herts

Bandler, R (1985) *Using Your Brain for a Change*, Real People Press, Utah

Conner, D R (1993) *Managing At The Speed of Change*, Random House, New York

Covey, S R (1999) *The 7 Habits of Highly Effective People*, Simon & Schuster, London

Csikszentmihalyi, M (1991) *Flow, the Psychology of Optimal Experience*, HarperPerennial, London

De Botton, A (2005) *Status Anxiety*, Penguin Books, London

Frankl, V E (2004) *Man's Search for Meaning*, Rider, London

Gilbert, D (2006) *Stumbling on Happiness*, Harper Press, London

Green, A (2005) *Out of the Blue*, Paragon Publishing, Rothersthorpe

Kabat-Zinn, J (2005) *Wherever You Go, There You Are: Mindfulness meditation in everyday life*, Hyperion Books, New York

Mellott, R (1995) *Stress Skills for Turbulent Times*, Careertrack Audiotape, Careertrack Publications, Boulder, CO

Peck, M S (1990) *The Road Less Travelled, a New Psychology of Love, Traditional Values and Spiritual Growth*, Arrow, London

Rinpoche, S (1998) *The Tibetan Book of Living and Dying*, eds Patrick Gaffney and Andrew Harvey, Rider, London

Robbins, A (1992) *Awaken the Giant Within*, Simon & Schuster, London

Taylor, R and Humphrey, J (2002) *Fast Track to the Top*, Kogan Page, London

Tolle, E (2005) *The Power of Now*, Hodder & Stoughton, London

Tzu, L (1999) *Tao Te Ching, an Illustrated Journey*, trans Stephen Mitchell, Frances Lincoln Ltd, London

Yapko, M (1997) *Breaking the Patterns of Depression*, Doubleday, New York

Note: only fragments of the writings of Heraclitus still survive, but there are many websites that will give you more information.

INDEX